AUDREY HEPBURN

An Intimate Portrait

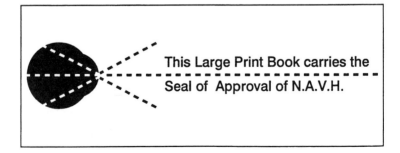
This Large Print Book carries the
Seal of Approval of N.A.V.H.

AUDREY HEPBURN

An Intimate Portrait

Diana Maychick

Thorndike Press • Thorndike, Maine

Published in 1994 by arrangement with Carol Publishing Group.

Thorndike Large Print ® Basic Series.

The tree indicium is a trademark of Thorndike Press.

The text of this Large Print edition is unabridged.
Other aspects of the book may vary from the original edition.

Set in 16 pt. News Plantin by Ginny Beaulieu.

Printed in the United States on acid-free, high opacity paper. ∞

Library of Congress Cataloging in Publication Data

Maychick, Diana.
    Audrey Hepburn : an intimate portrait / by Diana
Maychick.
      p.   cm.
    ISBN 0-7862-0103-7 (alk. paper : lg. print)
    ISBN 0-7862-0104-5 (alk. paper : lg. print : pbk)
    1. Hepburn, Audrey, 1929–   . 2. Motion picture
actors and actresses — United States — Biography. I. Title.
[PN2287.H43M38 1993b]
791.43′028′092—dc20   93-42995

For my husband, David Foote, with love and gratitude for showing me the way.

Audrey Hepburn

For all her chic thinness, she had an almost breakfast-cereal air of health, a soap and lemon cleanness, a rough pink darkening of her cheeks.

— Truman Capote,
Breakfast at Tiffany's

Acknowledgments

Look at all the wings in my midst!

There is no doubt that Audrey Hepburn is the prettiest, sweetest angel in heaven, but I want to thank her for sharing so much of her time on Earth with me. What else can I say? I miss her tremendously.

My sincere thanks, too, go to my guardian angels of late, the two Kevin Mc's: my agent, Kevin McShane, and my editor, Kevin McDonough. They know just how much I relied on them, and I want you to know, too.

I am also grateful to Fifi Oscard (founder of the literary and talent agency of the same name) and Steven Schragis (founder of Carol Publishing), the bosses, respectively, of my guardian angels. These two wonderfully smart human beings also have a touch of the celestial about them.

This book would never have been completed without my best friend, Blanka Nedela, who offered her prodigious research skills to give me a jump start, and catered a magnificent wedding party when my marriage and my deadline coincided.

For "three hots and a cot" during a particularly grueling period of writing, I wish to thank my mother, Stella Maychick, whose unflagging devotion and enthusiasm have always seen me through the dark times.

Among Audrey's peers, I want to express my heartfelt gratitude to all who spoke with me, especially Gregory Peck, Billy Wilder, Stanley Donen, Albert Finney, Shirley MacLaine, and Peter O'Toole.

The entire staff of the beleaguered New York Public Library was most helpful in finding long lost articles about Audrey, as was the staff of the Ferguson Library in Stamford, Connecticut, most especially Marilee Tremlett.

A number of colleagues deserve mention: Carol Publishing's director of publicity, Ben Petrone, for suggesting the book in the first place, and *New York Magazine* columnist Jeannette Walls for recommending me. Thanks, too, to Alvin H. Marill, Tom Cherwin, and Tony Vargas, and the editors at Sidgwick & Jackson, my publishers in the United Kingdom, Trijnie Duut, my editor on the Dutch version of the book for Luitingh-Sijthoff, and the Public Broadcasting System's John McKinley.

For their love, companionship, and encouragement, I wish to thank all my friends and family: George and Arlene Foote, Gary, Cathy, Jessica, and Adam Foote, Richard, Judy, and Beth Foote, Pia Lindstrom, John Parsons, Carol Bradley, Lauren Krenzel, Fabienne Marsh, Jay Butterman, Elli Wohlgelernter, and all my feisty aunties: Lucy Kettell, Sally Burney, Claire Ferraro, Bobbie Ashton, and the late Mary Kindt and Helen Lanzano.

Finally, to my husband David Foote, for not only putting up with me while I tried to write my first book as an ex-smoker, but for actually having enough faith in me to propose marriage in the middle of it all. Thanks for the vote of confidence, and also for printing out endless revisions!

Foreword

When I first signed the Birch Lane Press contract to write a book about Audrey Hepburn in March 1992, I never dreamed that she would provide me with such unprecedented access.

All I can say is that from the moment we first talked on the telephone that month, Audrey Hepburn and I clicked. I reminded her we had met five years earlier, when I was a theater columnist for the *New York Post* and anxious to do some good in the world. At the time, I was a volunteer at Bailey House, New York City's first hospice for AIDS patients, and Audrey had recently signed up as the ambassador-at-large for UNICEF. We met at a benefit at the United Nations, and we didn't talk about film at all. We spoke about trying to help other people without being too intrusive on their privacy.

When I told her I was planning to write a biography of her without being too intrusive, she said, "Can't be done." I figured she meant the book couldn't be done at all. What she actually meant, as I learned in the months ahead, was that the book couldn't be done unless she was willing to share some intensely personal, intensely painful memories. She did so unflinchingly and with great honesty.

During the year, we spoke intermittently, sometimes for as little as ten minutes, sometimes for as long as an hour and a half at a stretch. If Audrey didn't want to talk about something, she would say so, and I would drop the subject. That changed around Christmastime. She was more chatty than ever before and she seemed to relish our conversations. Nothing seemed off-limits. Of course, I had no idea she was dying, but in retrospect, I wonder if this was why she seemed so forthcoming. About that time, I proposed coming to Switzerland to speak to her at her home in Tolonchenaz. She sounded agreeable to the idea. We put off any further discussions until after the holidays.

When she died on January 27, 1993, I was on a spiritual retreat outside of San Francisco. I had no news from the outside world. When I boarded the plane to come back to New York, the woman sitting next to me asked me what I did for a living. "I'm a writer," I said. "What are you working on?" she asked. "I'm in the midst of a book about Audrey Hepburn," I said. "Isn't it a shame?" the woman remarked, and tears came to her eyes.

Even when she told me the news, my eyes remained dry.

For several weeks, I couldn't believe she was actually gone. We'd never had a proper final conversation. There were so many questions that would be forever left unanswered. I became despondent for a while.

Then I remembered Audrey telling me she looked on the bright side of things. "It wasn't always that way," she said. "I had to grow into this philosophy. Grow old into it!"

I realized how lucky I was to have spoken to her at all. I realized how wonderful and warm and supportive she had been of this project. Then I started to cry. I missed her. I knew I would never again hear the phone ring and her melodious, soft, lilting voice say, "Hello, Diana. It's me, Audrey."

Chapter 1

She had no idea even how cold it was, except for the fact that her paper-thin fingertips were already turning blue.

All she knew was that for the last month, she had kept warm by keeping going. She was running around town from after-theater parties to acting classes to afternoon teas in her honor. There ladies who usually lunched skipped their meal to ogle her figure, one disparaged, at least at the beginning of her career, by men used to the pinup curves of Marilyn and Jayne. But Audrey was so busy, there wasn't even enough time to search for her heavy sweaters in the top shelf of the closet of her furnished apartment. Just keep going.

March 25, 1954, was an uncommonly brisk evening in Manhattan. Winds ruffled theatergoers in midtown Manhattan as they hurried out of the Broadway houses trying to beat one another to the few available taxis in Times Square. Men holding on to their homburgs teetered on curbs and motioned for cabs. The weather pleased a number of their escorts, charter members of the generation who still wore minks and sables as a badge of pride.

But as they were stroking their pelts, they noticed that Audrey didn't even have a coat. Reed-thin, with a neck that recalled Modigliani, she exited the stage door of the 46th Street Theater and walked to the main entrance, where the white Rolls-Royce was waiting. She had the same fishnet dress she had worn onstage. The wind seemed strong enough to blow her down, but she pushed against it, and she won. She was stronger than she looked.

The hired limousine deftly pulled away from the curb and negotiated a path through the crowded streets. Pedestrians who watched her get in that night just assumed that Audrey was pampered by her driver, at least to the extent that he'd heated the car to a perfect temperature before her arrival.

Nothing could have been further from the truth. The driver had no idea at all who his scrawny passenger was or why she merited so luxurious a mode of transportation. Although in the last month she'd received rhapsodic reviews for her performance in Jean Giraudoux's *Ondine*, she had not yet become a celebrity. Despite critical acclaim for *Roman Holiday*, few had yet seen the William Wyler dramatic comedy. Like the driver, most people had no idea who Audrey Hepburn was. Sure, they read the *New York Herald Tribune*, but mostly the sports pages and the household hints, so most of them had missed what Walter Kerr said about her there: "She is every man's dream of the nymph he once planned to meet."

The only reason the driver even opened the door for her is because she whimpered about being unable to do it herself. Her hands had become paralyzed in the cold.

Racing across town to the Century Theater for her first Academy Awards show, Audrey bit the tips of her fingers to regain feeling in them. She had awakened that morning — as she had every morning in New York for the last couple of weeks or so — having forgotten that she was the toast of the town. It was her first sustained encounter with fame, and it "unnerved me considerably," she said later. "I was too young really to have had a firm grasp on who I was before all the attention. Then with all eyes on me, I became extremely self-conscious. My mother helped me to see that the attention was a boost to my career."

As soon as her hands defrosted, she flung aside the blond wig she had been wearing nightly as a water sprite, the title character of Ondine in the stage fantasy.

Until the opening of the Giraudoux play, Audrey had comfortably taken refuge in the idea of being a perennial student — studying dance, taking acting lessons, improving her voice range. But now that her show was a success, and she was up for an Oscar in her first big movie, she felt a bit like an impostor. As she finger-combed her unruly dark bangs, she felt she was getting ready for her next performance. She adjusted a few bobby pins in her hand-done bun. There was no time to fuss, let alone to think.

In a few minutes, she'd be escorted into the Century Theater, where she'd be expected to sit serenely dead-center orchestra. It would be an acting job of supreme will, given that she would be flanked by the two people she loved best — her mother, the Baroness Ella van Heemstra, and her future husband, actor Mel Ferrer — who had lately revealed themselves to be one another's mortal enemies. She was expected to sit quietly and regally in her gown and await news of the winners of the Academy Awards from Hollywood, where the show was being simulcast from the Pantages Theater.

That night, Audrey was on the verge of becoming an international star, and she could barely contain herself while waiting for the results. At twenty-four, she had captured the hearts of theater-goers. The film industry had already anointed her a shining light, thanks to an Oscar nomination for her first leading role.

Roman Holiday, the modern fairy tale about a princess who skips her stultifying royal obligations to pal around and sightsee in Rome with an impoverished, somewhat shady American newspaperman (played with brio by Gregory Peck), impressed audiences with its reverse-Cinderella theme. And as the princess who panted after life as a commoner, Audrey was one of the most charmingly believable royals in the history of the screen. You couldn't help but notice breeding and sophistication in her demeanor and hear boarding school in her voice, yet she desperately wanted to be just like you and me. The combination was an extremely winning one. Anyone who had ever felt like an outsider identified with the role.

Roman Holiday wasn't Audrey's first movie, but as her best and biggest to date, it gave viewers their first taste of her enchanting blend of impishness and regality. And that night in the grand white limousine, the young woman who had spent the war years scavenging for food like tulip bulbs and hiding from the Nazis actually felt just like Cinderella at her first ball.

"Most people think of Audrey as regal," Gregory Peck recalled. "But I saw how hard she worked at that. It was part of her heritage, yes, but circumstances — the war, her missing father — tarnished her crown. That was inevitable, but it was really a good thing. It rounded her personality. Despite her clearly recognizable look — what I like to think of as a sophisticated elf — she had a multidimensional personality. She had spunk. It took tremendous courage to tackle a leading role like Princess Anne [in *Roman Holiday*] without experience. But she plunged right in. I'm sure there was fear, but she didn't allow it to paralyze her. She jumped! It was really my wonderful good luck to be her first screen fellow. I didn't have to work too hard in that movie. I feel like all I did was hold out my hand and help her keep her balance while she made everybody in the world fall in love with her."

On March 25, 1954, two continents fell in love with her. It was a landmark evening for the retiring young actress who liked nothing better than to work hard all day, have a minuscule meal, and dive into bed to start memorizing her latest script. For the first time in history, London and Hollywood had scheduled their most important movie awards ceremonies for the same night.

As Audrey raced from the Rolls-Royce and

into the Century Theater, she was thankful that wooden horses and policemen helped keep her fans at bay. The movie crowd was especially exuberant, having learned moments before her arrival that Audrey had already won the British Film Academy citation as best actress of the year. They pawed at her, shouting their congratulations. It was at once exhilarating and suffocating. For a brief moment, she became scared. "I never dreamed I could elicit this much attention," she recalled, "and I must say, I didn't like it. In retrospect, I felt like a commodity. But at the time, I just wanted to hurry up and get dressed. I felt awfully foolish in that stage costume."

In the backstage dressing room, with the help of her ever-hovering mother, Audrey hurriedly changed into a sleeveless white lace gown and demure pearl teardrop earrings. She wiped the heavy stage makeup from her face and took off ten years. She looked about fourteen. "Hey, Skinny, hurry up," yelled a photographer impatient to snap her picture. She and her mother dashed to their seats, the matronly baroness excusing herself as she nudged past the other members of their row. On the aisle, Lena Horne blew a kiss to Audrey. Steve Allen and his wife Jayne Meadows commented to one another about how young she looked. "To see her in person that first time was a clear indication to me that Hollywood was up to its old tricks again. I was composing a little essay about cradle snatching in my mind," Allen said. "The only thing that looked legal about her was her eyes — and they were so deep, it was illegal." She sat stock-still in her seat, but what she really wanted to do was grab the hands of her mother and Ferrer.

Audrey's sultry competition that year intensified her image as an innocent waif. She was up against bona fide femme fatale Ava Gardner (*Mogambo*) and aspiring femme fatale Deborah Kerr (who did her best to eradicate her straitlaced image by rolling around on the beach that year in *From Here to Eternity*). Her other opponents were Leslie Caron, as a fetching orphan who joins the circus and falls in love with a magician (Audrey's fiancé, Mel Ferrer) in *Lili*, and another newcomer, Maggie McNamara, in *The Moon is Blue*, in an extremely suggestive role as a calculating young girl balancing the attentions of two lovers (played, coincidentally, by David Niven and William Holden, actors who would soon become Audrey's close friends). *Moon* outraged the censors by flouting the Production Code. Up against all of these sexually suggestive performances, Audrey's insouciant charm seemed unbeatable.

She and Kerr were the only Best Actress

nominees to appear at the New York ceremony, as they were both currently appearing on the Broadway stage. Emcee Fredric March oversaw the New York production, and Donald O'Connor was host of the Los Angeles ceremony. They teased one another in a novel split-screen technique that had been perfected especially for the event. "Hi, Dad," the younger O'Connor greeted his older counterpart in New York, who bridled at the dig.

Gossip on both coasts that night centered on Hollywood's favorite shaky marriage — Ava Gardner and Frank Sinatra. Columnist Army Archerd had reported they were splitting up, and Gardner's absence that night, despite her nomination, did bespeak domestic trouble. So did Sinatra's "dates."

Nominated for Best Supporting Actor for his role as Maggio in *From Here to Eternity*, the onetime idol of the bobby-soxers brought along a couple of his kids from his first marriage, Nancy Jr. and Frank Jr., to keep him company at the Los Angeles show. "Don't ask me anything," pleaded Sinatra's producer, Buddy Adler. "I'm not responsible for what I say. I don't know what I'm doing." Adler was nervous Sinatra might say something demeaning about Ava Gardner.

According to Oscar chroniclers Mason Wiley and Damien Bona, Sinatra-watchers were treated to a lot of fatherly behavior from the crooner, who seemed engrossed in his children. In a move calculated to garner sympathy from proponents of family values, Sinatra gave an interview to Hedda Hopper designed to portray himself as a model father and paragon of Catholic virtue. "The minute my name was read," he said after his Oscar win, "I turned around and looked at the kids. Little Nancy had tears in her eyes. For a second I didn't know whether to go onstage and get it or stay there and comfort her . . . I got Nancy a little miniature thing for her charm bracelet, an Oscar medallion. The kids gave me a Saint Genesius medal before the awards, engraved with 'Dad, we will love you from here to eternity.' Little Nancy gave me a medal and said, 'This is from me and St. Anthony.' That's her dear friend. She seems to get a lot done with St. Anthony. I guess she has a direct line to him."

In truth, the kids fidgeted a lot and seemed a little bored with the whole affair. Adults had various affairs of the heart and other matters to keep themselves occupied. Presenters Elizabeth Taylor and her husband, Michael Wilding, appeared to vie with each other for the shortest haircuts of the evening. Best Supporting Actress nominee Grace Kelly showed up on the arm of her *Mogambo* costar, Clark

Gable. Folks wondered about their relationship, but wondered more about a newcomer named Kim Novak, who, according to gossip columnists, posed as provocatively as Marilyn Monroe for anyone who cared to look.

Even though she had to view most of the hoopla on a monitor, Audrey was getting an overwhelming dose of Hollywood excess. Curiously, she'd admit later, while she recoiled at the vulgar display of phoniness and pretension, her mother seemed to enjoy the overblown affair. For the Baroness, the glamorous ritual of Oscar night represented the security of having made it in a new country. For Audrey, it meant the beginning of competition with her peers, which she always loathed.

Laconic leading man Gary Cooper, on location in Tijuana for a film, was asked to present the Best Actress award. He had filmed the sequence long in advance. "Folks down here in Mexico are just as excited," he said, as he ripped open an envelope and pulled out a blank sheet of paper. "Shall I read it?" Donald O'Connor asked from Hollywood.

Fredric March stepped onto the stage in New York and announced, "The winner is — Audrey Hepburn!" Her victory had been expected by everyone except Audrey herself. At that moment, her charming inexperience revealed itself like a blinding smile. She darted up the aisle, taking the steps to the stage two at a time, and then in her excitement completely lost her sense of direction. She turned left instead of right, and nearly walked off the stage into the wings. The audience roared. Was she also a comedian? Audrey righted herself and pranced back to center stage, making a self-deprecating little face to the audience, as if to say, "Please forgive me. I'm a little out of my mind tonight." She nearly knocked March over in her enthusiasm. "This is too much," she said, by way of thanks.

"I meant that," she said years later. "It was too much. I was a dancer really until that night. Until I won, I thought of myself as a dancer who acted. The Oscar changed all that. And I don't know that I was really ready for that."

In fact, she was completely unprepared. On her way to the press conference after the ceremony, she lost her Oscar and was unable to pose for pictures until somebody provided her with a substitute. "They found mine later in the ladies' room," she said. "I must have left it there after I looked in the mirror and realized how awful I looked."

For the rest of the question-and-answer period, Audrey's behavior was wildly out of character and overly demonstrative. She kissed onetime actor and Academy president

Jean Hersholt on the lips.* When she was asked how she planned to celebrate the evening, she giggled and said, "At home with Mother." In fact, she and Ferrer dropped the Baroness off and joined Deborah Kerr and her husband for drinks at the Persian Room at the Plaza. "It was a pleasant evening," Ferrer recalled. "We were really a bunch of theater people laughing at the contrivances of Hollywood."

Three days later, Kerr would stop laughing as Audrey beat her again, winning the Tony Award for Best Actress. In the history of the Oscars and the Tonys, only one other actress had received both honors in the same year. That happened the year before, when Shirley Booth captured both for Arthur Laurents's play *The Time of the Cuckoo* and the movie of *Come Back, Little Sheba*, based on William Inge's drama. But Booth was already a seasoned veteran of the stage; Audrey was a newcomer.

Although she shrugged off her acclaim because she really didn't believe in the artifice of awards, some of her peers interpreted her response as disdain — or worse, ingratitude. "From the moment of my first success, people got the wrong idea about me," Audrey said.

* Decades later, in 1993, she would posthumously be given the Hersholt Humanitarian Award at the Oscar ceremony.

"And a number of people never really bothered to figure out that although I had great respect for the art and craft of acting, I never really cared for the business. They thought me inconsiderate. The fact is, I cared too much, but only about the things that really counted."

And unlike so many of her peers, Audrey always knew what they were.

Chapter 2

The most startling news is that she was a chubby baby, with fat cheeks and roly-poly thighs, and a tummy that protruded from her organdy pinafores. She was as round then as she would be thin later, transforming into the svelte mannequin who made extra flesh seem vulgar. But when she was little, her dimpled knees drew praise.

Edda Kathleen van Heemstra Hepburn-Ruston, the name on Audrey's baptismal certificate, was born on May 4, 1929, in Brussels, and from the moment she came wailing into the world, she exhibited an enormous appetite. "Mother always said I was forever hungry," Audrey recalled. "I drank more milk than my two [half] brothers put together, but apparently, I was never satisfied."

It may well have been that even as an infant, Audrey was attempting to compensate with food for what should have been forthcoming in love. Long before the term was current, it was clear that Audrey was the product of what we now call a dysfunctional family. Class

29

differences between her mother and father only added to the domestic turmoil, as did the presence of Audrey's two half brothers, Alexander and Jan, offspring of her mother's first marriage.

Audrey's mother, Baroness Ella van Heemstra, never forgot that she was born into a long line of Dutch nobility and, despite her fluctuating bankbook, never let anyone else forget it. Raised in The Hague, the center of political life in the Netherlands, Ella spent vacations, occasional weekends, and every summer at the ancestral estate at Doorn, in Utrecht, the smallest of the Dutch provinces. The central castle was surrounded by a wide moat, which Ella used to think of as her private river. Thousands of tulips could be seen from her window and she learned the rudiments of arithmetic by counting the flowers. In this idyllic setting, nannies and maids indulged Audrey's mother, who never had to lift a finger. She would have a difficult time taking care of herself later when her circumstances changed drastically.

According to Audrey, Ella's own mother was aloof, spending a lot of time overseeing the running of the household, but her father shamelessly spoiled the child, giving in to her every whim — except for one.

"My mother desperately wanted to become

an actress," Audrey recalled. "Yet my grand-father strictly forbade her to go near the stage. He was adamant. He felt the occupation was beneath his daughter, and might reflect badly on the van Heemstra heritage. I don't think my mother *ever* got over her disappointment in obeying him." Her encouragement of Audrey's career — some would call it the un-relenting pushiness of a stage mother — is perhaps more understandable in light of her own thwarted ambitions.

Ella never fully recovered from her father's edict. By the time she was twenty, she had come to realize that she was supposed to marry, and marry well, and again she acceded to her father's wishes. The "good Dutch boy" she agreed to wed, the Honorable Jan Hendrik Gustaaf Adolf Quarles van Ufford, Knight of the Order of Orange-Nassau, turned out to be snobbish and exacting in private, someone who rarely enjoyed an unscheduled moment in a life devoted entirely to upholding the monarchy. From the start, Ella often argued with her husband, failing to accept that she was meant to be subservient to her mate, and that her wishes were not immediately granted.

In the first three years of her marriage, she attempted to leave her husband three times, but each time her father persuaded her to try to work things out for the sake of their two young sons. In 1925, after five years of marriage, Ella could stand it no longer, and she was granted a divorce. The public disagreements between the couple and their final rift scandalized Ella's family, and may have contributed to the van Heemstras' move to Suriname.

The Netherlands' Queen Wilhelmina had offered Ella's father a diplomatic post of his choosing, and the fact that the Baron had decided upon the underdeveloped, primitive, South American country that was bordered by the Orinoco and Amazon rivers reinforces the idea that he welcomed getting away from judgmental eyes.

As governor, the Baron enjoyed the perquisites attached to the post, especially the deference shown him by the English inhabitants of the commonwealth, who overlooked his daughter's unseemly divorced state and invited Ella to all their parties when she visited with her two sons. It was during these extended vacations that she began calling herself "Baroness," a title to which she was entitled, but one that struck many of her South American friends as a bit pretentious.

During one trip to a nearby island, she met Joseph Victor Anthony Hepburn-Ruston, an ordinary-looking banker of English-Irish descent who made up for his looks with a personality that could charm even the disillusioned Ella. He lavished attention on her, handpicking orchids to make a bouquet, and wiring back to the Continent for the silk scarves she missed and the satin bed jackets she decided she could not live without. Given his slavish devotion, there was no doubt Joseph was the man for Ella. Even the Baron, who had previously disdained any non-Dutchman who came calling, saw immediately that Joseph catered to Ella's desires and would indulge her in the manner to which she'd become accustomed, and gave his blessing.

The trouble was, Joseph expected to spoil Ella with her own money. Hepburn-Ruston's decision to live off his wife was just the first indication that their relationship would not run smoothly. Another cause for their marital discord was the move to Brussels. Ella found the stolid, bourgeois atmosphere of the Belgian capital stifling in the extreme.

From the beginning of their courtship to the end of their bitter marriage, Audrey's mother and father displayed a prodigious disregard for anyone but themselves. Their incessant squabbling took its toll on the only child they had together. "There wasn't much time for me," Audrey recalled. "And in some ways, I guess I missed the early attention for the rest of my life." An extremely willful woman, Audrey's mother was clearly inhibited by the stifling attitudes toward women at that time, particularly in Brussels, the stately city of Audrey's birth and perhaps the most straitlaced of all European capitals. "My mother would have been better off in Vienna, or anywhere in Italy or France — anywhere where music and art were of equal importance to food and drink," Audrey recalled. "She stood out a little, just a little, in Brussels, because her interests appeared frivolous. You've got to realize that even the aristocracy of Belgium is basically bourgeois. My mother's minor rebellions made her something of an outcast."

Yet Audrey strongly identified with her mother, and was also perpetually torn between conventionality and creativity. They remained unusually close until the Baroness died in 1984, often sharing the same home, and when not, speaking on the phone every day. The Baroness was the single most important influence in Audrey's life, certainly more powerful than any of her husbands or lovers, and her overbearing personality had a devastating effect. An extremely private person, Audrey refused to publicly admit the damage, but friends and relatives acknowledge that the Baroness kept tight control of her daughter, and inadvertently encouraged Audrey's latent eating disorder.

For most of her life, Audrey had a love/hate relationship with food. As a toddler in Brussels, on the secluded estate her father owned before his marriage, she so enjoyed the ubiquitous Belgian chocolate that her mother told the kitchen help to hide the candy bars to prevent her daughter from gorging.

"Chocolate was my one true love as a child," Audrey said. "It wouldn't betray me. I've always said it was either chocolate or my nails in those years. There was a lot of anxiety." While living at her mother's family's home at Arnhem during World War II, after the Nazis forced her into hiding, she nearly starved to death in a dark cellar, and felt twinges of survivor's guilt for the rest of her life. "Why was I spared when so many others were not? I asked myself that over and over, and I always tried to find an answer that wasn't there."

Having survived near-starvation, food became a luxury to Audrey, not a necessity. Save for a few tulip bulbs and dirty rainwater, she had done without it for a month. In her mind, she didn't need it. For the rest of her life, in times of great stress Audrey would just stop eating. Like many women with eating disorders, it was her way of attempting to exert power over her problems.

Then there was her mother's tendency to be overweight. As controlling as the Baroness was in most areas of her life, she could not get a handle on her weight, and spent most of her life trying to hide twenty-five excess pounds. She blamed her size for a host of problems, including her husband's roving eye. Audrey noted how unhappy her mother was and, at least subconsciously, also attributed it to her weight. She made a vow to herself never to exceed 103 pounds. With the exception of her pregnancies, she succeeded. But the cost was sometimes enormous.

As a child, Audrey was always trying to keep things together, to make them perfect in the hope that her parents would stop fighting. "I often thought that if I could be a better daughter, pay more attention to the rules, get to the dining room on time, Mother and Father would have less to worry about. But I was a big daydreamer, and I forgot my promises as soon as I made them." She also read the Bible religiously, as a sort of penance to make up for her nonexistent sins, and promised baby Jesus she would do anything he asked as long as her parents stopped fighting.

She was also just a child, too young to realize that her parents' incompatibility was not her fault. Her father, Joseph, born in London in

1889, came from a financially comfortable family, but he always had to work for a living. His relatives were commoners. Audrey's mother would put him down for his relatively humble roots whenever they fought about money, which was their major area of disagreement. Like the Baroness, who was twelve years his junior, Joseph had been divorced before their union, and felt an overwhelming social pressure to make his second marriage work.

Finances interfered from the start. On September 7, 1926, they married in Jakarta, where the Bank of England had stationed Joseph as an investment counselor. The Baroness was eager to return to Europe, but the bank was not ready to transfer Joseph home until he had paid his dues at one of their less important outposts like Indonesia. The Baroness intervened, and won. She persuaded her father to allow her new husband to manage his money, thereby insuring his swift return to the Continent.

In Brussels, where the family settled, Audrey's father became the managing director of the Belgian branch of the Bank of England. He had lamented returning to Europe so soon, having learned to enjoy the freer lifestyle of Jakarta, and he began drinking rather heavily. "My father was in over his head, my mother said," Audrey recalled. "He wasn't really up to the responsibility of his job or his instant family. Don't forget, he inherited my brothers, and they were rambunctious young men. He had his hands full."

Her half brothers, Alexander and Jan, virtually ignored their baby sister and spent their days in the rolling hills behind the tall, gray Brussels house shooting slingshots at birds and roughhousing with one another. Practical jokes were another favorite diversion and Gerda, their beloved and long-suffering cook, was often the brunt of their teasing. She took the blame for them when their jokes backfired, including the time they broke a priceless hall mirror and their baby sister cut her thumb. They were muscular boys, full of adolescent energy, and the Baroness didn't encourage them to include their baby sister in their exploits.

That was just the way Audrey liked it. Unlike her robust, hale Dutch relatives, she was a retiring child who liked to retreat into her room with a book. With no childhood friends to speak of, she was perfectly content to be alone, and happier still in the company of animals. Audrey felt uncomfortable only at dinnertime, when the family convened around an old, heavy mahogany table and her mother would start picking on her father.

Their jabs at one another were relentless. By 1931, her father began spending more and more time away from home with his boss, Mantagu Norman, the governor of the bank in London. Norman introduced Joseph to his circle of pro-Nazi friends, including Unity Mitford, a good friend of Hitler's, and the sister-in-law of Sir Oswald Mosley, the figurehead of the Fascist movement in England. The group began meeting regularly in support of Nazism. Audrey's father was in complete support of Hitler and eventually joined Mosley's Black Shirt Brigade. Joseph often came home spouting all sorts of hateful propaganda, and the children became fearful of his raised voice. "I still loved him, though," Audrey said. "I loved my father more than any other man in my life."

When he left the family, he instilled in Audrey a fear of abandonment that she would never outgrow.

Chapter 3

Life in the Hepburn-Ruston household became as quiet as a monastery after Audrey's father left in 1935 and moved to London. But the relative peace belied the inner turmoil Audrey was experiencing over the breakup of her family.

"I never played with dolls," she said. "Mother would often lament this fact, since I was her only daughter and she liked the idea of my dressing up the things and combing their awful blond hair. But the real reason I didn't like them is that I felt I had to play house with them, and I didn't want to bring up all the pain of what my own home life was like. We went from loud screaming matches that were never resolved, to utter silence, like a cloistered existence. It was extremely perplexing. It hurt too much. I didn't want to talk about it. I preferred to ignore it."

She also began to eat away her sorrows, counting on a chocolate bar or afternoon pastry to ease her loneliness. "It was a frighteningly awful time, especially since I refused to tell anybody how low I was feeling. There I was, just about six years old, and I know now I was clinically depressed."

What gave Audrey a sense of hope — and made her smile for the first time since her father left — was going to the ballet with her mother. "She began by taking me to concerts, which I adored. I remember hearing Mozart for the first time and thinking that there was a glimmer of hope. Life finally offered up a good surprise. Music! I felt good while I listened. Then she began taking me to the ballet, and that was even better. For that hour and a half, I forgot my troubles. I got lost in the sheer beauty of bodies moving in time to music."

Soon, Audrey's extreme shyness and reserve started to crack a little. She began expressing interest in something other than her fantasy world of perfect families. She told her mother she wanted to take up dance.

"Mother was ecstatic," Audrey recalled. "Not only was I fulfilling one of her secret desires to go on the stage, she also hoped I'd lose some of my baby fat. A tummy had plagued her ever since she'd had children. Excess weight was looked down upon in her circle — it meant peasant stock. My mother was a bit of a snob, and the last thing she wanted was to perpetuate a legacy of fatties."

41

Curiously, her ballet lessons only served to encourage even more weight gain. "I wasn't really used to sustained physical activity," she recalled. "My brothers didn't play with me, and I had no close friends as a child. I wasn't the type to run and climb trees and hike the mountains either. So when I took up ballet, I developed an enormous appetite. After a class, it felt like there wasn't enough chocolate in all of Europe to satisfy me."

Looking back on that time from the perspective of adulthood, Audrey attributed her hunger to hidden feelings of inadequacy. "I was always berating myself for things that I couldn't change. So I ate to compensate.

"My teeth also used to bother me an inordinate amount of time, for example. They were crooked. In fact, they're still crooked, but I am used to them now. However, with orthodontia work, they could have been straightened. But that was never offered as an option when I was a girl. I don't think my mother thought it would be worth the expense, and I never asked her why. I didn't want to know really if she didn't value me as much as my brothers. In any case, there were so many things I, myself, couldn't change about myself, and they all conspired to make me feel inadequate. I suppose it all went back to my father leaving. After that, nothing felt right."

Audrey so missed her father that she persuaded the Baroness to allow her to spend as much time as the courts would allow with him in London. Yet it was nothing at all like what she expected. "He worked all day, went out with lady friends for dinner, and I rarely saw him," she recalled. "And I was jealous of everyone who did. I had this wonderfully prim governess for a while, extremely straitlaced, and I used to begrudge her the ten minutes a week she spent with my father discussing my progress."

At the day school she attended, she felt more like an outsider than ever before. Her classmates taunted her because of her thick Dutch accent, her poor command of English, and her thorough lack of interest in sports like field hockey. "For my whole life, my favorite activity was reading. It's not the most social pastime."

For the next couple of years, Audrey still harbored a hope that her parents would reconcile. "The only times they really talked was about me, so I figured if I gave them trouble, they'd have more and more communication. The trouble was, I was afraid of trouble. As much as I wanted them together, I was petrified of being naughty to achieve that goal.

I was definitely a 'don't rock the boat' girl, even though I knew that the more they had to talk about me, the more they had to talk."

Audrey still gave them both a lot to worry about, even if they each did their fretting alone. "I wouldn't talk at all for days on end," she recalled. "I think I was afraid that if I opened my mouth, I would start to cry. And I knew if I started to cry, I wouldn't be able to stop."

At the age of nine, while in her father's care, she began taking a weekly ballet class in London. Again, her perfectionism became obvious, but for the first time in her life, it began to work in her favor. "I was overweight, uncoordinated, awkward, and sloppy. My sense of timing was off. Yet by sheer will, I did well," she recalled. "It was the one thing that held me together when my parents' divorce came through."

In mid-1938, three years after filing the papers, the marriage of Baroness Ella van Heemstra and Joseph Hepburn-Ruston was officially dissolved. Although the Baroness rarely laid blame, she would obliquely allude to her ex-husband's involvement in the pro-Hitler Black Shirts as the contributing cause. But Audrey herself discovered later that her father may also have mismanaged the van Heemstra fortune he was entrusted with upon his marriage. "There were even whispers about embezzlement," Audrey said. "It made me suspicious of men's motives when they professed their love. I was always wondering if they were after my money."

Despite the bitterness of her parents' split, they still were aware enough of reality to recognize that their daughter was the true casualty of the episode. Guilty about the effect of their failure on their little daughter, certain that she was being torn apart because she loved them both, they agreed that a London day school would be a good temporary solution. It would at least postpone the decision about which parent Audrey would live with the majority of the time, and remove her from the endemic family depression which often accompanies divorce.

Against all predictions, Audrey thrived away from home, at least on the surface. She developed a ruddy complexion from joining in outdoor team sports with her classmates and began to catch on a little to the steps required in making friends. By now fluent in English and French, Audrey appeared to be the model child of an upper-class, European upbringing. In fact, she began suffering severe migraine headaches at this time, most probably a result of her inability to acknowledge the pain of her family life. Still, what she learned in those few short years would stay with her for the rest of her life: You could keep your unhappiness a secret, and nobody would be the wiser. You could hide your feelings to keep them under control.

Then, in the autumn of 1939, the world started spinning out of control.

Chapter 4

Life was about to change dramatically and irrevocably, but as in those moments before every cataclysm, people in the maelstrom remember best the mundane.

"What pains me the most is the way the students made fun of me when I returned to the Netherlands," Audrey says. "I really didn't know much Dutch even before I left, having spoken English at home, but by the time I got back, there was nothing. And even when I tried, my accent was awful. Children can be mean and hurtful. I felt completely alone."

In September 1939, the Baroness insisted that Audrey leave her father in London and immediately come back home to Arnhem. England had declared war on Germany, and Audrey's mother was certain that Hitler would attempt to invade the British Isles. She was extremely nervous about her husband's pro-Nazi stance, and feared that his politics would adversely affect her daughter if she were allowed to remain in London. In her view, the

Netherlands would continue to exist as a safe haven, no matter what happened in the rest of the world. She had the assurances of Queen Wilhelmina herself, who often exchanged confidences with the Baroness's sister. Despite the fact that Arnhem was less than fifteen miles from the German border, the Baroness brought Audrey back home to live with her half brothers Alexander and Jan.

For a child still distraught by the breakup of her parents, the sundering of the world around her was just a footnote to her internal pain.

"I was crying a lot of the time when I first got home," she recalled. "I would sit and whimper and eat chocolate and try my best to learn Dutch. There weren't too many distractions. I learned the language by default. There was nothing else to do."

The Baroness tried to cultivate diversions for her sad little girl, but the tensions of the war inhibited fun. Instead of outings, Audrey spent most of her days poring over books about ballet stars Pavlova and Nijinsky in the wainscoted library of the family estate.

She became an avid balletomane, immersing herself in the rituals and lore of the dance world. The magical transformation of a body into an instrument for art helped distract Audrey from the pressing concerns of food, clothing, shelter, and safety.

Safety had become an important issue almost overnight. In the spring of 1940, Hitler was massing his troops for an assault on the Netherlands. By this time, the Baroness had become the unofficial leader of the Dutch Resistance movement in her hometown. Her ex-husband's reprehensible beliefs in Nazism initially encouraged her in this opposite direction, but soon the Baroness herself became enamored of the Underground, and devoted countless hours in planning strategies.

The estate of Arnhem became a center of the clandestine movement, with the Baroness throwing informal parties which helped to swell the ranks of the opposition. Royalty mixed with commoners at these afternoon and evening affairs, and everyone shared ideas. For perhaps the first time in her life, the Baroness realized that beliefs were more important than class distinctions. A romantic air washed over each ordinary occurrence. People spoke in codes. Life was tinged with a do-or-die excitement. Commonplace conversations resonated with deeper meanings.

"I don't remember what all the things stood for," Audrey said, "but I do know that if someone mentioned rijsttafel [the Dutch national dish of fish, meat, vegetables, and subtle spices], that meant there were lots of ears around and listening! You were supposed to be careful of what you were saying; somebody in the room could be a Nazi sympathizer. We all had to be very secretive until it was clear whose side our neighbors were on. And since the Dutch are known to be rather close to the vest anyway, we often were surprised when we discovered other resisters. Some of the most laconic people worked the hardest for the cause."

For the Baroness, fighting the Nazis also functioned as a subtle way of getting back at her ex-husband. Although she didn't encourage Audrey to bad-mouth her father, she did press her young daughter into becoming a zealot against Hitler. Audrey's father's support of Oswald and Diana Mosley and the reactionary Fascists only grew more intense as the years passed. Whereas in his early days he quietly offered financial and moral support to the infamous Black Shirts, he now marched with them in public parades. "My loyalties were divided," Audrey recalled. "Even at age eleven, I knew Hitler was evil. But my father supported him. And I loved my father. I prayed that my father would change his mind, and then maybe the family could get back together. I think for the rest of my life I prayed that my family could get back together."

During a period of extreme political tension,

on the night of May 17, 1940, the Baroness decided to take Audrey to the ballet to see one of her idols, Margot Fonteyn, who was visiting Arnhem with the esteemed Sadler's Wells Ballet. The wonderful English company, under the tutelage of choreographer Ninette de Valois and musical director Constance Lambert, also featured dancers Robert Helpmann and Frederick Ashton in a repertoire which included Ashton's own "Horoscope," the story of young lovers ruled by their astrological signs. During the performance, the dancers got word that Hitler's troops were nearby. They realized that they should leave Arnhem immediately.

Performing a truncated version of "Façade," which was danced before a set featuring the outside of a beautiful, stately Victorian mansion, the troupe rushed through the various components, skipping a waltz altogether in the hopes of saving time.

But the Baroness had other ideas. As the president of the British-Netherlands Society, she used the visit by the Sadler's Wells Ballet to shore up her image in the Resistance movement.

Knowing there were more than a few Nazi sympathizers in the audience, and knowing, too, that they were beginning to doubt her cover as a pro-German aristocrat, she wanted to make it appear she was trying to detain the troupe long enough for the Nazis to arrive. That would help create an aura around her as being on the side of Germany. She needed such an ironclad alibi to continue her secret work in the Resistance movement.

In order to prolong the evening, she got on the stage and thanked the ballet troupe in English and Dutch. As the dancers were becoming more and more nervous and uncomfortable, the Baroness began to review the history of Sadler's Wells, recalling nearly every one of its triumphs, including the minor ones. Desperation began to color the faces of the dancers. Fonteyn was said to turn ashen. Helpmann swooned as if about to faint.

The troupe was becoming even more anxious. The Baroness feared they would leave while she was still talking. That's when she publicly initiated Audrey into the Resistance movement. She motioned her daughter to bring to the stage elaborate bouquets for both Fonteyn and de Valois. Audrey walked slowly and regally up the carpeted aisle, curtsied flawlessly for each woman, and whispered to them that she herself wanted to become a dancer. "It's what I dream about every night," she told them, clutching a dog-eared program in her sweaty palms. The dancers were so touched by her wide-eyed charm and quiet poise that they persuaded their fellow dancers to stop by at the reception the Baroness had arranged in their honor.

A half hour after the troupe got onto its bus and left, the Germans noisily blasted the streets of Arnhem. Air-raid alarms screeched warnings of danger. The sound of gunfire punctured the quiet night. Parachutes filled the sky. Audrey and her mother returned home and slept in the basement, where Alexander and Jan and their nanny had already found refuge.

"It was for me a most amazing night," Audrey said. "I was too exhilarated about meeting Fonteyn to be as frightened as I should have been about the war. It was almost as if the bombing started and the shooting became constant because I had screwed up my courage and told my idol that I wanted to be a dancer just like she was! The sounds were like fireworks to me, an affirmation that I had desires and I finally voiced them. Oddly enough, I think my depression began to lift that night. It wasn't until morning that I realized it was damp in the basement, that there were mice and even rats, that I was shivering. All those things were true, and I began to feel them, and the fear of death, but everything was also finally all right. I had discovered a purpose in life. I was to become a dancer."

The invasion changed daily life dramatically and quickly for Audrey and her family. Radio reports urged civilians to stay inside and lock their shutters and doors. "My brothers and I peeked out the windows and saw the German soldiers, a sea of gray really, in their uniforms and with their guns. It was a menacing sight, but somehow I felt we could beat them. It was a child's boldness, I suppose, a naïveté. It became like a game. But when the Queen left [Wilhelmina and her family went to England to wait out the war], we felt abandoned. The leader had decided not to play with us anymore."

In the week that followed, bullhorns blared the news that Arnhem was now part of the Third Reich. The city's radio station and its newspaper were under the control of the Germans. The Baroness helped to organize a strike against the railway system to slow down the German invasion. Some Resistance members were caught and executed by the Germans as an example of what would happen to those who resisted.

Audrey's family was financially decimated. The aristocracy, of which they were leading members, had suffered great losses. All their gold was confiscated, and their silver money was replaced by zinc. The van Heemstras lost all their wealth and property. The Germans commandeered their Arnhem house as a sort of headquarters. Although they were permitted to remain there, they became unwelcome boarders in their own home.

But by far the most devastating event for Audrey was the arrest and execution of her mother's brother, Willem. "It is still hard for me to talk about my uncle," she remembers. "I didn't see him every day, maybe no more than twice a month, but he was an anchor in my young life. He wasn't a substitute father, but he was an adult male who loved me, who loved my mother."

A prominent attorney whom the Baroness had persuaded to join the Resistance movement, the elder van Heemstra was arrested by the Nazis for blowing up a train carrying German soldiers. In a public display of barbarity, he was placed before a firing squad in the town square and executed along with five other Resistance fighters.

The Baroness was distraught over her loss, but she continued to fight. Even after her brother's son Frans was arrested, she still held meetings in her basement and encouraged her friends and neighbors to sabotage the gestapo. But when her nephew was then executed by the Germans, she went through a harrowing night questioning her own motives.

"She cried for hours," Audrey recalled. "I

had never seen my mother display emotion before, let alone cry. But she seemed to get out her anguish a little by wailing uncontrollably. That's a funny way to say it, right? Wailing is, by nature, uncontrollable. But I was so used to seeing my mother in charge, taking care of things, making them right. To see her lose her senses frightened me beyond measure. I made up my mind I would take care of her from then on. And I realized almost intuitively that the best way to do that would be to let her think she was taking care of me, that she had to be strong to make sure I would pull through."

So began a lifelong pattern of appearing weak so that others might be able to feel superior. Audrey would do anything in order to insure a connection with others, because she often didn't feel quite at home with herself.

During the war years in Arnhem, her imagination worked overtime at concocting a fantasy life that completely supplanted her real one. For days on end, she lived only in her mind, seeming not to notice that food and water were running out and that the dwindling supplies were becoming contaminated. "I guess I began to resent food around this time," she said.

"That's a strange thing to say about food

56

— 'I resent it.' You eat it, don't eat it, like it, dislike it. But resent it? I actually got angry with it for being so difficult to come by and tasting so awful. I decided to master food; I told myself I didn't need it. I could sense it caused my mother great pain not to provide my brothers and me with the well-balanced and beautifully served meals she was used to, so I felt I could eliminate her problem by denying I missed the good things we used to eat. Of course, I took it to an extreme. I forced myself to eliminate the need for food. I closed my eyes to the fact that I was starving."

The protracted nature of the war made matters much worse. "There was this overriding sense that the Occupation would be over very fast," Audrey recalled. "Nobody could conceive of the long, slow, drawn-out tragedy of war inflicting its indignities every day. No matter how depressed people became, we all believed it would be over tomorrow. Every miserable day, we still thought it couldn't go on like it was. So part of me thought to myself I wasn't starving, I was fasting to end the war."

Yet life became inexorably more difficult. At the Arnhem School of Music, where Audrey was studying, all composers who were not German or Austrian were banned from study. Jewish teachers were fired. The German language became mandatory. Any remnant of Dutch nationalism — a pendant, a pin — was forbidden.

Audrey became a quiet rebel. While she seemed to acquiesce to Nazi rule, she worked ceaselessly to raise money for the Resistance, sometimes giving donation-driven ballet recitals in the homes of sympathizers to meet her own self-imposed quota.

In a curious way, dance functioned as a useful trade in those dark days. In her mind, Audrey was pirouetting to save lives. It elevated an idealistic young woman's artistic avocation into an important, patriotic duty. There was no applause. The sound of hands clapping would have been too dangerous. Figuratively speaking, performing arabesques was now a mission of resistance. If she wasn't completely hooked on a life in the theater before the war, the days of deprivation forced Audrey to recognize that art also had a profound healing power. It fed her soul.

Because her Dutch was still rudimentary, it became too dangerous for Audrey to continue her classes at the school in Arnhem. Her difficulties with what the invaders assumed was her native tongue would raise all sorts of questions about her lineage. According to her mother, several generations back she had a Jewish ancestor. The Baroness had always been extremely proud of her mixed heritage, but the specter of Nazism made her much less vocal about her genealogy. She began to fear for her daughter's life.

Audrey began to study alone at home, with a tutor coming in once a week to drill her in mathematics. The subject bored her until the teacher started to use practical applications to help spark her interest.

"I have always had a reputation for being frugal — less kind people might call me cheap. But my interest in building up a nest egg goes back to those days in Arnhem when I learned that money can grow, just like trees."

As she was learning more about personal finance, her mother and the rest of the van Heemstra clan were becoming progressively more impoverished. When civilian food rations were restricted, and more and more Nazis began bunking down at the Arnhem home, the Baroness decided to move her family to a more modest house on the outskirts of town. She hoped it might be possible to grow some vegetables and raise a few chickens to feed Audrey and Jan.

A year earlier, the older of Audrey's two half brothers, Alexander, had been taken away to a German labor camp near Berlin when he refused to join the Nazi *Jugend*, or youth movement. Audrey was so distraught over the separation from her brother that she refused to talk about him, or even mention his name.

"When I was little, Alexander had introduced me to some wonderful adventure books, most memorably Kipling, and I would often bring his 'Just So Stories' into the basement and pretend he and I were characters.

"I developed a tendency to retreat to a fantasy world when life wasn't going my way. Although I never talked about Alexander to my mother or to Jan, I talked to him all the time. I promised him I would never marry if he returned safely and that I would take care of him, cook and clean, for the rest of my life. Can you imagine how desperate I was?" Audrey recalled, laughing. "I also made bargains with God. For a quiet thing, I was chattering in my head all the time."

Yet such anguish paled in comparison with the atrocities she witnessed every day during the German Occupation.

"On a fairly regular basis, although I can't tell you how often because I've blocked it, I would see families being taken away, jabbed by rifles until the babies would be screaming and the mothers begging to be killed if only their children could be set free. They would be loaded onto wooden train cars, thrown in there sometimes with such force you could hear the bones break," she said quietly.

"There was very little air to breathe. You could hear people gasping. The sound of that was so frightening, I would begin to gasp, too. I developed asthma soon after, and no matter how many doctors tell me it's not connected, I know that my breathing problems were influenced by those poor souls I didn't even know.

"The families always looked so downtrodden, no matter who they were. I saw the baker, a jolly man, so hunched over when he was being taken away that he was half his real size.

"The women were the ones who were usually carrying more. I suppose they just couldn't bear to leave behind the family mementos — photographs, a small silver frame. One woman was fingering a set of expensive buttons. It seemed to me she was planning to sew them onto a new coat for her husband when they got to their destination. Everyone seemed to try so hard to maintain dignity. But the spouses were often separated at the station. Of all the tragedies, this one struck me the hardest: that people who loved one another, families, could be pulled apart when they needed each other most."

Audrey developed a sense of outrage at man's inhumanity to man that would remain with her for the rest of her life. She also learned in these early years that she could offer the most help in intolerable situations by quietly trying to change them. "I was never a screamer," she said. "I always got the most accomplished by acting docile and sweet. I always looked like such a good little girl, and I always used that image to my advantage."

After seventy Dutch schoolchildren, some of them her friends, were sent to prison for attempting to blow up Nazi cables and gas lines, her efforts in the Resistance movement redoubled. While her mother continued to pose as a pro-German Dutch aristocrat, Audrey became increasingly aware that she could accomplish wonders if she played up her naive schoolgirl persona, complete with a feigned indifference to the tragedy around her.

It was a stellar performance. Here was a child who ate only a few leaves of endive and a potato a day, and who skipped merrily through the town square as if she had not a care in the world. Inside her worn-out shoes, however, were coded messages for Resistance workers. On the pretense of playing in the fields, she often veered off into the woods and shared her potatoes with the pilots of Allied planes who had been shot down in her area. Bouncing a ball higher than usual, she would use its landing as an excuse to go into a neighbor's yard and boldly hand him some anti-Nazi pamphlet which explained how he could aid the cause.

In 1942, Audrey tested her acting abilities to the limit and gave what she always considered to be the performance of her lifetime. Her mother had sent her on a dangerous mission to make contact with a British paratrooper who had safely landed in the forest on the outskirts of town. Her command of the English language made her a highly prized messenger.

After she had fulfilled her duties, she saw out of the corner of one eye a German soldier coming toward her. Out of the corner of the other, she saw the paratrooper squat behind a rock. "It was all a matter of seconds," she recalled.

"But I knew I must appear carefree. That was the word: carefree. I'll never forget it. So I bent down and picked a clump of daisies immediately; I pulled so hard I got them by the roots. But I thought they would add to my look. By the time the German got close, I had my head in the flowers and was pulling the petals out one by one. When I pretended to see him for the first time, I smiled casually, as if I were distracted, but I certainly didn't look frightened. I offered him the bouquet. He took it, patted me on the top of my head, and I hopped away."

Closer to town, she winked at a street sweeper. That was his signal that he would have an Allied soldier to hide in his home that night. She winked again and smiled and skipped away.

She would not be so carefree for long.

Chapter 5

In 1943, Audrey's world diminished and became more desperate. The dangerous game she was playing as a participant in the Resistance became more tenuous as the Germans tightened their stranglehold on Arnhem.

Approximately one in ten Jews living in the Netherlands was aided by a Dutch compatriot in finding a hidden shelter or fake identity. Anne Frank was only one of thousands of brave unknown souls who used every ounce of strength to survive, and sometimes did not.

Audrey continued her secret work in the Underground, and because her fluency in English was so useful, she found herself at the forefront of the Resistance effort. She was also adept at forging signatures on identity cards, able to imitate a flowery, cursive hand as well as a messy scrawl. She would carry these important documents to the people whose lives depended upon them in the soles of her shoes, in a false bottom in her bicycle basket, sewn into the lining of her coat.

"Life then was a struggle, but it was also

very rewarding," she recalled.

"I loved the subterfuge. What child wouldn't? Of course, the work was frighteningly dangerous, but I never thought about it at the time. That's the beauty of a child's perception. I can recall lots of whispering. It seems all we did was whisper and make funny hand signals and eyebrow lifts and scratches on the head, touching the left meaning something different from the right, and a tap on the cheek meaning something else entirely. At the time, the signals were indelibly etched on my brain. I felt like I could never forget them. Of course, I did."

But the naive excitement of a girl living the pages of a spy novel was tempered by an increasingly bleak mood in the van Heemstra household. The Baroness was suffering from a severe depression, one that would recur intermittently for the rest of her life. Distraught from the moment she had learned that her son had been sent to a Nazi labor camp in Germany, Audrey's mother was nearly catatonic after two years went by and there was still no word about Alexander's fate. She became totally aloof from Audrey and Jan, investing all her dwindling energy in fighting the enemy and privately mourning the loss of her son. Her cover as a Nazi sympathizer was beginning to wear her down even further.

She began to hate the effort it took to lie. Lack of food had also reached a crisis situation.

"Jan was the most hungry," Audrey recalled. "That was clear. He'd sometimes hold his stomach and cry for food. I couldn't stand another minute of it. I suppose Mother was hungry, too, but she was too sad to notice. I, on the other hand, was sure I wasn't hungry. I thought I had that one beaten. The only thing I knew was that I had to take care of them, so I devised this outlandish plan to make money."

In the middle of the Occupation, with a blanket of gloom beginning to suffocate all of Europe, Audrey decided to give ballet lessons. She would take a trolley from her temporary living quarters in the countryside to the town square, where she'd walk a few blocks to the Arnhem Conservatory of Music. The decrepit tutu in her satchel shared space with a pair of ballet slippers so worn and patched, they resembled heavy quilted material rather than delicate satin. Her students were young girls much like herself, stuck in Arnhem for the duration of the war. Some were Nazi sympathizers, some resisters. Audrey didn't care: They would be paying her to teach them to dance.

Although they looked up to Audrey for her stoicism in the face of disaster and her finely tuned ballet technique, some of the cattier members of the class must have made snide remarks about her painfully bony look. Audrey was totally emaciated.

Her standard starvation diet of lettuce, an occasional potato, and an awful bread made of peas got even worse when that food ran out. Audrey would live on tulip bulbs and water until she could secure potatoes again. She weighed less than ninety pounds, she was continuing to lose weight, and she was exhausted.

"Everybody was painfully thin, at the School of Music and everywhere else in Arnhem," she said. "I wasn't alone. But since I was leading the class, I had to repeat certain movements at the barre over and over for some of the slower students. I had just performed a series of pliés, when I felt all the blood rush to my head and then — blackness!

"When I came to, one of the janitors was chastising me about not eating. I can still see his wagging finger, not pointing with recrimination, but with love. He took me into a large supply closet, brought down a box from the middle shelf, and took out a red ball of Edam cheese.

" 'I was saving this for a real emergency,' he said. 'Well, you are it!'

"Just a small piece revived me; I tried some

more but became sick to my stomach. My body chemistry had changed during the years of deprivation, but my mind was also playing tricks. 'If there is no food,' I had said to myself, 'then I'm not going to need what I can't have.' It was one of my first attempts at mind over matter, and at the time, I thought I was doing a great job."

In fact, malnourishment forced Audrey to stop dancing for a while. There would be no more *Swan Lake* or *Nutcracker* to transport her into that place of serenity. She still continued to act as a courier for the Resistance, but the Nazis had stepped up their efforts to catch spies, and Audrey lived in a perpetual state of anxiety.

Her trepidation was warranted. Despite years of beating the odds, on a quiet summer day in 1944 Audrey faced the monster she had so luckily avoided for so long. The gestapo had been beefing up its efforts to provide Germany with slave labor, and on that day in Arnhem was rounding up women to cook and clean in military camps and prisons.

From a half block away, Audrey saw friends and acquaintances being forced at gunpoint to get into trucks that would take them to places worse than hell.

"There was a girl I knew in passing from the library at the Conservatory. She had a red scarf tied around her head. She was standing in a group of women — all ages — huddling, it seemed, against the intrusion of the German soldiers.

"The red scarf! I used to see that scarf next to her books all the time when she was studying. It was a comforting, familiar sight. Now I saw her being pushed with the butt of a rifle into a truck. A woman with a limp, whom the Nazis did not take, was trying to pull back this girl. I presumed it was her mother. In those few seconds, I wished the girl would give her mother the scarf.

"I did not want that red square of pretty material to wind up a ripped and soiled rag in a labor camp. Tears came to my eyes. If I think about it now, I was grieving for the loss of this girl, this human life. But that was too much for me to acknowledge at the time. I just wanted the scarf to be safe and sound."

The Nazis had other ideas. As Audrey was watching the girl she knew in passing being taken away, a gruff officer hit her in the small of her back with his rifle. In German, he commanded her to follow him to a new group of women being assembled in the same spot from where the others had just been driven away.

"As we walked, he right behind me, with his rifle sticking in me, I tried to keep my head held high, with dignity. I kept my satchel on my shoulder, refusing to drag it and look beaten. But I noticed all the shopkeepers, the street cleaners, the bus conductors, they all looked at the soldier with utter contempt. Their hatred was obvious, and useful. I knew then that no matter what happened to me, we would win — in the end, we would win."

As she joined a few other women at the site, her captor and all the other Nazi soldiers but one left to gather more victims for enslavement.

"The soldier left behind was extremely young, self-conscious. He seemed ill at ease around girls, even one as scrawny as me. At one point, he put down his rifle against a lamppost, pulled a tobacco pouch from his jacket, and began to roll a cigarette. He was all thumbs. He was concentrating hard not to spill the tobacco and make a fool of himself."

It was Audrey's only chance. She took it.

The emaciated young teen with arms and legs so bony she was painful to look at, who suffered from anemia, edema, and the preliminary stages of anorexia nervosa, ran for her life. She rounded a corner before the awkward young soldier even realized she was missing, and then she fled down an alley. Toward the end of it, she ran down a few steps and forced open the door to an abandoned cellar.

Inside, she found a few empty crates, lots of yellowing and decaying newspapers, and the constant sound of scurrying. "Rats were everywhere, it seemed, but they were my only company, so I made up my mind not to be afraid."

Audrey remained in that cellar prison for nearly a month. "That's what I was told, anyway. I have no real concept of days passing during that time. I was in and out of consciousness, I guess. I had a few apples in my bag, and a little bread; that was my food. I tried to sleep a lot to avoid the hunger pangs. But in the times I was awake, I would try to hum some music in my head. I wouldn't make a peep, but I would try to hear violins and pianos and the beautiful sound of the cello. The war had made a prisoner of my body, but my mind was my own. And even in those circumstances — especially in those circumstances — I wanted to enchant it."

When the sound of gunfire got closer, Audrey decided to leave. "I can't really explain that decision, except to say that hearing the sound of guns at least lets you know you are alive!"

Barely able to walk, she slowly limped out of the cellar dungeon and made her way home. She is not sure how she did it.

Her tearful reunion with her mother left the

Baroness speechless. "She was so certain I'd died that it was hard for her to comprehend the sight of me. I know I looked like a ghost anyway! A yellow ghost."

Audrey had contracted hepatitis during the three-and-a-half-week exile, and suffered from the withering effects of jaundice. She also began wheezing while in hiding, and her breathing difficulties were later diagnosed as asthma. Her metabolism, always speedy, would now never adjust itself. And she would, in later life, always refuse to eat during stressful times.

"I associate food with happy times, primarily because those times when I was unable to eat were so miserable. I guess in some convoluted way, I'm afraid if I eat when I'm sad, I'll be feeding the sadness," she said.

The period before liberation and the end of World War II was an especially desolate one for Audrey. She had exchanged her private dungeon for a familial one — she, her mother, and Jan fled to their basement when the Battle of Arnhem began.

By late summer 1944, American and British forces had liberated most of France and Belgium. It was time to push closer to Germany. Arnhem, on the Rhine, was chosen as a perfectly situated city behind enemy lines in which to drop thousands of airborne troops to begin recapturing territory.

In early September, the Baroness heard rumblings among her underground Resistance circle that something was about to happen.

On September 17, more than eight thousand soldiers from the First British Airborne Division, the famous Red Devils, were parachuted into a three-square-mile area to try to take control of the road bridge at Arnhem. The Germans were ready for them.

"The noise of the first landing was unlike anything I had ever heard," Audrey recalled. "You could hear the screams, the sounds of the brave Allies being killed while they were still in the air. We were in the basement, and it sounded like there would be so many bodies when we finally surfaced that we'd be unable to walk for fear of stepping on them."

The Baroness took in other townsfolk who were afraid to stay in their homes nearer to the bridge. On the day after the initial invasion, nearly forty people were sleeping on the floor right beside the van Heemstras. Arnhem itself looked like nothing less than an extremely active slaughterhouse. Mangled bodies, some still tangled in their parachutes, lay everywhere, while evacuees from the west arrived in record numbers, hoping to find refuge.

"There was not enough food," Audrey said.

"Don't I sound like a broken record? But that's a wild understatement. There was no food at all. Oh, we managed to get some black-market flour to make a gruel for all our houseguests, but the stuff was full of bugs. Actually, we were secretly all delighted: It was the first protein any of us had had in a long time.

"And by this time, everybody had learned to share. War forces people to be magnanimous. It's the one good thing. Six slightly injured airmen landed not far from where we were living, and Mother took them in. Thank heavens the underground network was still operating, even though its ranks had been diminished. We heard the gestapo was coming to make a surprise inspection. We had to hide the men, so we put them in Mother's big closet."

Five of the men were able to leave soon after; the sixth, Lt. Col. Anthony Deane-Drummond, remained with the van Heemstras for another two weeks, hidden in a smaller closet until he was fully recovered.

Allied reinforcements arrived in the next several days, but because the weather was foggy, they were late, and the Germans were again ready for them. More than seven thousand soldiers were lost in the weeklong battle at Arnhem, and the residents themselves were suffering equally devastating losses.

The Nazi leaders had ordered the majority of residents to leave Arnhem to prevent German soldiers from starving. The town's downtrodden citizens mingled with the recently arrived penniless refugees in a chain of human misery. Everybody wanted to get out. Roads were packed with the sick and dying carrying their infants, whatever warm clothing they had left, and a few pitiful possessions.

According to eyewitness reports, they cried as they walked, some silently, some with a wail of desperation. Deathly ill patients were released from hospitals and forced to crawl. Pregnant women gave birth at the side of the road. This was the war invisible to the outside world. This was the war at home, the battle for life of ordinary citizens who just happened to be caught up in the crossfire of soldiers. Of the estimated ninety thousand people who left Arnhem, three thousand died.

Audrey and her family lived far enough away from the center of town to avoid the enforced exodus, but they certainly were not immune from the further ravages of the Occupation. Soon after Lieutenant Colonel Deane-Drummond left to go back to England, the house in which Audrey's family was living was bombed. The impact of the explosion was so great that nothing survived. Thankfully, the van Heemstras were out trying to help their less fortunate neighbors at the time. They escaped the blast with only the clothing they were wearing.

Looting was rampant. German soldiers stripped houses of their silver, linens, fine furniture, and paintings, sometimes burying their booty in hopes of returning after the war to collect it. The road bridge over the Rhine was completely destroyed. So, too, was the medieval town square.

"We arrived at friends of Mother's whose house was still intact," Audrey recalled. "I guess there were only about two hundred or so houses throughout the area that were not razed. So where we were was very crowded. Jan was so quiet; I remember that vividly. I don't think he said a word during that whole long trek to yet another safe refuge. There had been so many, and none of them were safe. We were vagabonds. I wonder if he thought that's the way it would be for the rest of his life — just wandering from one place to another, avoiding tragedy by the skin of our teeth."

While they were at their latest way station, the van Heemstras barely averted another deadly mishap. The Germans had installed a radio transmitter on the third floor of the house in which they were staying. When the

British discovered the telltale electronics, they immediately suspected that the inhabitants of the house were collaborators.

"Don't forget, my mother had spent every one of the war years pretending to be a Nazi sympathizer. So when the British soldiers stormed the door with their long guns pointed at us, I calmly told them the story. 'Your English is so good,' they said, 'we've just got to believe you.' They all pulled out packets of cigarettes then and lit up. Freedom to me smelled like English cigarettes."

In April 1945, Audrey heard from a friend who had access to a radio that the Allied forces were on their way to Arnhem. The news spread fast. Emaciated and ill, the townsfolk defiantly came out of hiding to greet their liberators. Audrey was among them.

The Germans surrendered on May 5. When the British soldiers assembled again, this time to sweep Arnhem for deadly mines, Audrey helped them, giving them tips about the terrain of the countryside. Skin and bones, she refused to let the liberators out of her sight. Years of being forced to fend for herself had helped erase some of her shyness. "Thank you," she said to the soldiers. "Thank you so much for saving my life." She even kissed a few in gratitude.

The family soon had a personal victory to

celebrate. As the Baroness was mending some embroidered linens that she had managed to hold on to during her peripatetic war years, she saw a thin, tall young man hesitantly walk up the cobblestone path. She put down her sewing and went to the door.

"The whole scene took place in utter silence," Audrey recalled. "Words would have ruined it." The surprise homecoming of Alexander van Heemstra, the Baroness's eldest child, was the answer to the family's prayers. Although he had suffered unspeakable tortures in the German labor camp, he was strong enough at the end of the war to walk all the way home.

Audrey always attached great significance to her sixteenth birthday falling on the day before liberation. "So what if my present was a day late?" she would ask. "I got the greatest present in the whole world. And the end of the war was the greatest present to the whole world!"

She was so happy, in fact, that she actually wanted to eat. While working in a rest home for Dutch soldiers in an effort to repay her compatriots for their sacrifices during the war, she received a cache of milk chocolate bars in gratitude for her solicitude. "I ate all of them at once," she said. "Seven total. And then I got sick. I wanted to eat all of them, actually felt I deserved all the candy ever made, but then I felt guilty. Too many scenes of the war were still with me. They'd always be with me. Anytime I got too happy, there they'd be."

Her initial exhilaration at the end of the Occupation was marred by flashbacks of her more gruesome memories. "It was never really over, not if I had nightmares and daydreams about the torture. That astounded me. I could never get rid of this war. I had to live with it.

"But then I tried to make the best of that. There was nothing else I could do, save for self-pity, and that never got anyone anywhere. So I used what I witnessed to form a philosophy of life. It's simple. I saw people die, I saw loved ones separated, I saw cruelty and hunger on a daily basis. All that proved to me that nothing is more important than empathy for another human being's suffering. Nothing. Not a career, not wealth, not intelligence, certainly not status. We have to feel for one another if we're going to survive with dignity."

Chapter 6

Now that safety was no longer a pressing concern, the bare necessities of food, clothing, and shelter became the major hurdles for the van Heemstra clan. They moved to Amsterdam, hoping that a new place would offer a fresh start.

Jobs were scarce. The Baroness took work as a cook, maid, and housekeeper for a family whose pedigree was minor compared to her own. But the job came with housing, which was a major consideration. The family lived in a dank basement apartment below the big house. Psychologically, the adjustment from aristocracy to working class was devastating.

The Baroness had lost everything during the war, but now that the war was over, she felt these losses more acutely.

"Mother became maudlin remembering a painting or a candlestick from the old house," Audrey said. "She didn't have time to get nostalgic during the fighting, but once things were calm, there was time for regret. It was one thing to sacrifice during a crisis, quite another to realize you had to sacrifice for the rest of your life."

Audrey decided that in the long run, she could best ease the financial burden if she improved her only skill, so she got out her dancing shoes and began taking classes with Sonia Gaskell, an innovative Russian teacher who incorporated jazz and Latin rhythms into her classes.

"Mother and I were some pair at the end of a day," Audrey said. "I would get home exhausted, utterly spent, aching all over so much that I usually skipped dinner. Mother would be tired, too, from cooking and cleaning all day. But there was a certain perverse satisfaction in concentrating on our goals. Mother was trying to earn enough to support my lessons and I wanted to excel so that I could support Mother. There were no complications."

Except one. Audrey's teacher was not confident she could make a career as a prima ballerina. Although her technique was flawless, her teacher felt she was tall without being strong, a paradoxical aesthetic combination that ruined her look.

But she did impress a film director who stopped by one day. Charles Huguenot van der Linden was Audrey's Schwab's Drugstore, the man who first discovered the actress who would enchant the world for decades to come.

He arrived unannounced at Sonia Gaskell's class one day with the express purpose of finding a beautiful, brainless dancer who would fill to bursting a stewardess's uniform for a bit part in a travelogue he was shooting, "Nederlands in Zeyen Lessen (Dutch in Seven Lessons)."

Instead, he found Audrey.

From the moment the war ended, after a month of bedrest and force-feeding had eliminated her hollow look, Audrey captivated most everyone with whom she came into contact. At eighteen, she had already become the beauty who would enchant the world: doe eyes, aristocratic cheekbones, tiny waist and hips, regal carriage.

Her awkward, funny face was stunning now. Her perpetually startled look became startling. In photos at the time, she looked like a fawn in the midst of a seamless metamorphosis into a woman. The frightened wildness in her eyes was vastly appealing, so much so that director van der Linden decided to change his mind and cast against type.

In the film, Audrey was given two words to say: "Who, me?" It was a question that revealed her lack of confidence and one she would repeat for the rest of her life, although never more than in those early years of show business.

"I tried to get other films after that in Rotterdam, but I was turned down for all of them," she recalled. "It's not so much that I thought of it as a career, but more an easy way to make money. In lots of ways, that's what being an actress is all about. But in those very first years, I was still a dancer at heart."

Overwhelmed, driven, and frightened, she was determined to make good on all the sacrifices her mother had made to provide her with the dance lessons, the six-month season ticket to the Concertgebouw Orchestra, the series of Beethoven concerts. It was time for action. With her brothers off to the Dutch East Indies to try to find fame and fortune, Audrey decided to try to persuade her mother to move to London. Marie Rambert ran an important school for dancers in Notting Hill Gate, and Audrey was sure she could get a scholarship.

"Dire circumstances spurred me on," she said. "Looking back, I'm glad times were tough. If they weren't so bad, I wouldn't have been bold enough to push forward. I was always more introspective than outgoing, but when I really had to be, I could go after what was necessary. I was optimistic about my prospects, because the opposite was just too depressing. The truth is, I had no idea what I was getting into when I decided Mother and I should move to London. But I did think that changing my name would give me a boost. Edda had been through too much already."*

Mother and daughter arrived by boat with ten dollars between them. London, too, was still recovering from the war in 1948 and could barely feed its own, let alone immigrants like the van Heemstras. But Audrey and her mother had already proven they were from strong stock. They cheerfully washed and darned their two pairs of stockings each, aired their meager clothing after each wear to avoid dry-cleaning bills, and always looked ahead to brighter times.

The legendary Madame Rambert was sixty — wiry, eccentric, still dressed in black tights and her trademark veiled cloche — when Audrey became her pupil, but her energy and enthusiasm never flagged. She was an inspiration to Audrey, who worked harder than ever under her tutelage. But the young student also had practical concerns on her mind. The scholarship she had dreamed of did not provide for food, clothing, or shelter, and Audrey

* In fact, Audrey Hepburn was known by her given name, Edda Hepburn-Ruston, until she moved to England at age eighteen. For the sake of clarity, I have referred to her as Audrey Hepburn throughout the book.

and her mother again had a difficult time making ends meet.

"I worked for Mim [Madame Rambert's nickname] after classes and during lunch break," Audrey recalled. "She and her husband [Ashley Dukes] even took me in for several months to save on carfare. I think it was really just an excuse to feed me! Mother first got a job in a florist shop, where she met a businessman who helped secure her a position as an apartment manager in Mayfair. So she and I were climbing the ladder to independence slowly but steadily. I would do my chores for Mim and then rush off to audition in the West End. She went from one small room in her apartment complex to a real apartment. I don't think either of us could have done it without the other. We kept one another going."

In honor of their heritage, they used the decorative gold key from the family castle at Doorn as a knocker on the door of their modest apartment. But they didn't tell anyone about their once-exalted circumstances. "We had few friends," Audrey recalled, "and the ones we had were struggling just as much as we were. It is important, too, when times are tough, not to look back."

Madame Rambert had come to the sad conclusion that Audrey would not be successful as a ballerina. Although she was an eager student, her presence was too full of energy to be able to fade into the background when necessary. No matter what she did, Audrey could not fade into a troupe. Eyes were always focused on her.

"Mim didn't say anything to me," Audrey recalled, "which I'm forever grateful for. I guess I could sense that I wasn't up to par, but she never made me feel I was lacking. Oh, she still rapped me on the knuckles when my extension wasn't high enough, and she hurt! But she did that to all her students. A little corporal punishment in a field devoted to the body didn't seem so outrageous.

"She said very little, however, and words would have killed me if she had said aloud that I wasn't the right material. By keeping quiet, she gave me the chance to come to the conclusion that ballet wasn't quite right for me. But I didn't let that happen until I had something else to do in life. Otherwise, it would have been too devastating.

"Imagine persuading your mother to leave her homeland, find work and housing in a foreign country, sacrifice her own life for yours, and then find the bubble has burst! As much as I loved the art and discipline of the dance, it didn't love me!"

But as so often was the case, the situation

was not as desperate as Audrey had initially feared. Just when she had accepted the fact that ballet was not her metier, a regional troupe invited her to join it for an extended tour. Simultaneously, she received word that she was one of ten chorus girls chosen from among three thousand who'd auditioned for roles in the Jule Styne musical *High Button Shoes.*

The antic story of the adventures of a 1913 con artist, Harrison Floy, had enjoyed a long and successful run on Broadway before being brought to the West End.

Choreographer Jerome Robbins, today considered a genius of the stage, had arranged a number of extremely difficult, beautiful sequences for his "Bathing Beauty Ballet," the climax of the show.

"I remember going home after the audition and crying on my bed," Audrey said. "I had no idea about jazz dance steps and I had to remain stiff as a board just to get the sequences right. It's not that I even liked what I was doing! There was no comparison to ballet, which is an art form. But I thought it might mean money, which is something we desperately needed. I cried because I was sure I didn't have a chance."

She may have lacked expertise in the fields of jazz dance and musical comedy, but what

Audrey was missing in technique, she made up for with personality. Coproducer Jack Hylton captured her spirit at the time. After seeing her tryout, he wrote on a slip of paper: "Lousy dancer. Great verve." Verve would always carry Audrey when her mere mortal talents let her down.

Hylton signed her up on the spot. "He bellowed that I had the job," Audrey said. "He was so forceful that I didn't dream of telling him I had another offer in my real field. Besides, I finally accepted that I wasn't going to be a great big ballet star. I was being given an opportunity to try something new."

A few weeks into the run of *High Button Shoes*, British impresario Cecil Landau attended a performance and "was captivated by a girl running across the stage," he said. "It's hard to explain. It wasn't much. Just a pair of big dark eyes and a fringe flitting across the stage."

Anyone who saw Audrey in her earliest performances had a similar reaction. Here was a live wire, a broad-smiling, long-legged imp who just dripped with good breeding. Her effect was infectious; she got under people's skins and made them feel happy. She, too, was in a good mood. Hearing laughter every night from a packed house raised her spirits.

At nineteen, she had so far lived a frighteningly somber life, and this injection of levity was a real boon.

It was time for a change.

"Life as a chorus girl was a revelation," she recalled. "The ten of us shared a dressing room and I discovered for the first time in my life that I was a cutup. I loved to mimic people with funny accents and I had the girls laughing all the time. I was modeling for soap ads in my spare time. [Fellow chorine and future wife of Rex Harrison] Kay Kendall and I became friends. It was a wonderful time."

Audrey was on a roll. Cecil Landau offered her a part in his new 1949 revue, *Sauce Tartare*. She accepted the offer before even asking what she had to do.

The international musical travelogue, a kind of parade of nations on stage, required Audrey and four other dancers to cavort through a host of foreign capitals in skimpy costumes. The cast was international as well, and Audrey got to know performers from South Africa, Spain, Russia, Norway, Scotland, Portugal, and the United States. But their differences, and the often-impenetrable language barriers, slowed down rehearsals considerably. Landau, notorious for being blunt and often nasty, couldn't even lash out at many in his cast because they didn't understand him. He postponed opening night by a day and drilled his players for twenty hours without stop.

When the show opened, it was a resounding success. But Audrey was too tired to care. Throughout her career, she'd overdo efforts to please and wear herself out in the bargain. On her one day off, she slept for a full day and pretended she had been out shopping. "I always fought being delicate," she said. "It made me feel inadequate."

A year later, when Landau was casting for a similar revue, *Sauce Piquante*, Audrey was his first choice. "The audiences just loved her," he told a colleague. "With all the stars in the show, they always give that skinny little thing the longest ovation."

Moira Lister, the bona fide star of both revues and a comic actress renowned for her ability to completely transform herself into her characters, said that Audrey was "quite the opposite. She was herself whatever she did, and people just loved her for it."

Jealousies did arise, however. "I've got the best tits onstage," a buxom Scandinavian named Aud Johanssen reportedly griped, "but everybody's staring at a girl who hasn't got any!" Audrey always insisted the story was apocryphal, but she laughed with glee anytime it was repeated. "It's true," she said. "They did stare. But I think that's because I stuck out even more — in height, that is!"

Chapter 7

For a girl who kept to herself throughout her teen years, the heady experience of being watched and wanted was both intoxicating and frightening.

When famed photographer Anthony Beauchamp first laid eyes on Audrey, he "couldn't quite fathom that she was real. There were so many paradoxes in that face," he recalled. "Darkness and purity; depth and youth; stillness and animation. I had photographed many of the greats, Garbo included, but I felt I'd made a real discovery when I found Audrey.

"She had a fresh new look, a beauty that was ethereal. It certainly had nothing to do with her dancing. She was on the wooden side in that area, but she was so striking to look at, you barely noticed.

"She was extremely nervous when I approached her backstage after the show. I got the impression that a lot of gentlemen and not so gentle men were making her all kinds of propositions at this time. When I introduced myself and said I wanted to take her picture, she pleaded poverty. I told her the honor would be mine. I wanted to have her in my portfolio! After the session, she sent me a proper English schoolgirl thank-you note and a box of chocolates. She was one of the nicest subjects I ever had."

Critics, too, were beginning to single her out. "She had no lines to say, no part to play," recalled reviewer Milton Shulman about her performance in *Sauce Piquante*. "But with her infectious grin, she actually looked like she was enjoying herself. Perhaps it was this marked contrast to what the rest of us were feeling that made her as conspicuous as a fresh carnation on a shabby suit."

And the beauty of it all was that her delightful way, that charming insouciance, was a genuine reflection of her personality.

Dressed in tailored suits and pillbox hats, with her ubiquitous white gloves spotless, Audrey was the good daughter every parent longed for. And that kind of innocence embodied its own brand of sex appeal — she was the forbidden fruit, the unapproachable one. In fact, however, she was game for a variety of rough-and-tumble activity.

"I was doing a lot of modeling at the time," Audrey recalled, "and the photographers were always shocked that I was willing to take some risks for the photo shoot. I got a kick out of jumping across streams or hanging from the edge of a building. I wasn't afraid of stuff like that. After living through war, those things were minor."

But when one photographer suggested that she pad her bra to appear more bosomy, Audrey balked, until her press agent at the time, the influential Frederic Mullally, convinced her it would increase her wages. He kept a copy of the resulting ad and inscribed it "Audrey Hepburn — and friends."

The early fifties were the most delightfully free and easy years of Audrey's life. It was the first time she'd ever allowed herself enjoyment without worry. Her biggest indulgence was clothing; she got her first taste of couture while modeling for advertisements, and she finally began to appreciate her mannequin figure. She scrupulously studied her physical assets and liabilities and decided that pale colors and neutrals would best complement her sallow complexion. "Bright reds and blues tended to overwhelm me then," she said. Although her life was still circumscribed by work and her mother, financial security eased other burdens.

She became close to the cast and crew of *Sauce Piquante*, and they all started to socialize offstage as well. She no longer rushed home to the Baroness after her busy days of drama and dance classes, rehearsals, auditions, and nightly appearances in the show. But her well-rounded life offered new complications.

Marcel le Bon, the popular French singer and her costar, developed a serious crush on Audrey, becoming the first of many of her colleagues to fall in love with her.

"It was very innocent on my part," Audrey recalled. "Marcel would leave me sweet little billets-doux, nosegays, flowers, poems. He was the first man to pay this kind of attention to me and in the beginning, I was smitten more by it than him. Still, he was awfully kind. We had wonderful times together, but Cecil Landau worried that romance among his cast would ruin his show. He was a madman! He instituted a 'no-marriage' clause in my contract, can you imagine?"

There was also a twinge of jealousy on Landau's part. He opened a new revue, *Summer Nights*, at the landmark nightclub Ciro's, and fired le Bon even before the show opened.

The singer was so distraught he left for America. Nothing could have made the Baroness happier. She did not want her daughter settling down with an unreliable show-biz personality just as her career was taking off. In fact, she did not want her daughter to settle down at all, although that was all Audrey really wanted to do. The days ahead would be rocky ones for Audrey and her mother.

Chapter 8

Working in a nightclub seemed glamorous to Audrey. She loved the sound of glasses toasting and the scent of perfumes mixing in the air. She often stepped back from her life and looked at it with a sophisticated gleam of self-satisfaction in her eyes — but in her eyes only.

The only real indication that she was a woman of the world was the fact that she arose at ten. That was good enough for Audrey; she felt like a lady of leisure. No matter that she was a slave to show business from the moment she awakened until 4:00 A.M., when she would walk home from work exhausted and sweaty from the high kicks of the chorus line. The very fact that she could get up later than the average shopgirl, despite the reality that she worked longer and harder than most, meant indulgence and luxury to her.

Modeling jobs were especially plentiful. Audrey's gamine look impressed magazine editors as totally new. Her boyish beauty supplanted the standard images of glamorous artifice and hourglass figures long associated with high style. She was the real thing — a refined, naturally elegant brunette who exuded an inner warmth and vulnerability. It was the combination of these elements which made her look timeless and so impressed people who caught even a glimpse of her.

Actor John McCallum was one of them. One night he stopped by the floor show at Ciro's with his wife, Googie Withers. They were both so awestruck by Audrey's magnetism, they took it upon themselves to recommend her to casting director Robert Lennard. He was just as impressed with her ability to take command of a room, even when she was just one among many dancing girls.

Lennard also recognized that Audrey was the least talented dancer among her peers. He saw that she was flat-chested. He feared that her arms and legs might be on the verge of getting tangled up all the time. He wondered if she could actually be as skinny as she looked. Yet he also knew that she would be a star.

He persuaded friend and colleague Mario Zampi, a director of screwball comedies, to give Audrey the lead in his *Laughter in Paradise*, the story of a rich recluse who leaves in his will a fortune for each of his relatives — provided they perform outlandish, sometimes criminal acts.

Audrey met with the director and his screenwriter and she so impressed them, too, that a day later, they offered her the role.

But two days after that, she turned them down.

"I let my heart get the better of me," Audrey explained. "I often let my heart get the better of me!"

Back from America, Marcel le Bon, Audrey's first suitor, had begged her to collaborate with him on a new cabaret act, along with other alums of the Ciro show.

"I felt sorry for him. He had nothing going on in his career, and I thought I could help him. I had already committed to working on that little show when the movie was offered. So I wrote one of my nice and proper schoolgirl notes — a 'thanks awfully, but no dice' note.

"I wanted to work with Marcel," she said. "It was a very simple decision. We were going to do the cabaret brilliantly, get married, have babies, and live happily ever after. That was all in my mind. I was very naive. I didn't know too much about film, certainly not enough to think I was throwing away a big opportunity. I was at a time when opportunities kept presenting themselves, one after the other, boom, boom, boom. I didn't much discern among them. If one came and I passed it by, another would come. That's the way I thought.

"Well, reality intervened. Without Cecil behind us, the clubs took advantage. Our bookings fell through. I was shocked. People lied. It was a rude awakening. Marcel became angry. He took his disappointment out on me. We had terrible fights. And then he picked up in a huff for America."

Audrey was left alone, without a job. She did what she always did when she was up against a wall — she nudged up against it and tried to push it down, gently using all her strength. Little by little, it fell.

She humbled herself and went back to director Zampi, politely telling him that her circumstances had changed and that she was now free to do the job. Audrey was invariably, and genuinely, polite. She never lied or made excuses. People respected her honesty. But in this situation, there was little to be done. Zampi had already cast Beatrice Campbell in the role. But the director was still taken with Audrey.

"He told me he still wanted to use me, despite the fact that I had turned him down. He attributed that mistake to my youth, which in fact it was. So there were no hard feelings. When he offered me a bit part, I took it gratefully." Audrey had one measly line:

"Who wants a ciggy?"

Apparently everyone did. Her presence on screen was so strong that Associated British Pictures offered her a seven-year contract on the strength of her walk-on. It wasn't that people thought she was a natural actress, either. They recognized that she was awkward and self-conscious. But for some reason, they couldn't get enough of her.

"I thought it was the greatest gift," Audrey said. "Not because I had been dreaming my whole life of a movie career; I wasn't. In fact, I didn't see many movies growing up. The few that were available were Nazi propaganda pictures, and they didn't much endear me to the form. I loved the contract offer because it meant financial security. It was money I could count on. So you see, I got into a profession where you can count on nothing, ever, because it offered me security!"

For the next several years, Audrey worked steadily in English films. She had another walk-on as a hotel reception clerk in *One Wild Oat*, a farce about a spurned woman who tries to blackmail her former lover. Then she was cast in another light comedy, *Young Wives' Tale*, about the housing shortage in London after the war. Director Henry Cass remembered her as "beautiful, but inexperienced. I wasn't quite sure she would make it as an actress, although no matter what angle you saw her from, she was alluring. And she was the same offscreen as on. There was no difference."

It was the beginning of a long season during which Audrey would be courted by the world. At a party soon after filming, she met a strappingly handsome, tall, wealthy gadabout from Yorkshire, James Hanson, who was also impressed with her mesmerizing beauty.

"I remember him asking me where I got my eyes," Audrey recalled. " 'They came with the package,' I said. 'Well, I'd like to buy a whole carton of them to exchange with all the little squinty ones I see each day,' he said. 'I'd like everyone to have eyes like yours. It would make seeing so much more important.' Of course, I thought I was in love."

Hanson, who had a reputation as a ladies' man and who had been regularly escorting the actress Jean Simmons until he met Audrey, also fell head over heels immediately. At twenty-eight, after having served in the war in the Duke of Wellington's regiment, he felt it was time to settle down, and his wealthy father, the Huddersfield scion of a successful trucking firm, had agreed to finance a transportation business for his son.

"I loved the idea of finding a partner," Audrey said. "But it was just that: an idea. As soon as it became clear that I would have to give up the artistic and cultural life of London for an existence talking about golf and hunting and fishing, I was no longer so anxious to get married."

The Baroness adamantly opposed the alliance right from the start. She felt Audrey was too anxious to throw away her career for any man who came her way. Furthermore, she felt that Hanson would not be a loyal husband; she had observed him flirting with several of Audrey's girlfriends from Ciro's and was appalled at his boldness. She encouraged Audrey to dump him. Audrey wouldn't hear of it. She and her mother endured a tense period, one of the rare times they stopped speaking to one another.

She and Hanson, on the other hand, became inseparable when he wasn't traveling on business. Their romance was actually fueled by all the departures and homecomings. For a young lady who was usually reticent about making a show, Audrey seemed to thrive on the grandiloquent gestures of Hanson's love. She adored the roses and perfume, the public displays of affection at fox hunts and at performances of light opera. (He was a trustee of the D'Oyly Carte opera company, which had been doing Gilbert & Sullivan since 1881.) She shared the Swiss chocolates he showered on her with her mother, and generally enjoyed being the center of his world.

He was flamboyant, she quiet. But in the beginning, when their opposite natures were still getting to know one another, they appeared complementary. It was only after Hanson began resenting Audrey's career for interfering with their social life (she would often have to miss a cocktail party in Huddersfield, or a polo match at the club) that she began to see that their relationship might not work.

It was a possibility she admitted to no one, however. The very real breakup of her parents' marriage made Audrey extremely sensitive to implications, real or imagined, that she was not working hard enough to come to a compromise. For the rest of her life and in every relationship, Audrey felt that if she made the effort, she could force herself to get along with the man in her life. There was a price to pay. She would lose herself along the way.

Chapter 9

In September 1950, Audrey took another bit part. But this time it was in a film of considerable merit, the madcap comedy *The Lavender Hill Mob*. Once again, she was a cigarette girl, but selling the pack this time around to Alec Guinness proved fortuitous.

At this stage in her career, nothing seemed to go wrong. Other young actresses might have been disappointed at the relatively slow rise to fame. But Audrey had no real interest in adulation. She just wanted to earn enough money for herself and her mother, make more friends, and lead a useful life.

Although *The Lavender Hill Mob* was described as hilarious and Guinness's performance deemed brilliant, Audrey's role was completely forgettable.

Except to Guinness. He was so taken with her gazellelike neck and big brown eyes that he introduced her to the American director Mervyn LeRoy.

"I never remember Guinness recommending anyone else to me, before or since," LeRoy said. "Some actors are always working at connecting people. Guinness wasn't like that. He even said he didn't think she could act, but that she was so beautiful, so delicate, it didn't matter. Those are interesting words, coming from a consummate actor! It doesn't matter if she could act! I wanted to see this amazing creature myself."

Meanwhile, director Thorold Dickinson was finally given the go-ahead by Ealing Studios to get started on a movie totally unlike the light, romantic comedies upon which it had rested its reputation.

The Secret People was a serious movie whose theme was extremely close to Audrey's heart — the Resistance movement.

"It was the first film I wanted to do," Audrey recalled. "All the others were the froth on top of the beer."

The story involves two sisters, played by Audrey and Italian star Valentina Cortesa, who flee to London when their father is killed by a European dictator and who become increasingly involved in political intrigue and espionage as they attempt to avenge their father's death.

"It was the largest role I'd been given, and the whole thing was daunting," Audrey recalled. "The best thing about it was that I was more than familiar with the subject matter

— I'd lived it. That helped allay my nervousness. Another stroke of luck is that my character, Nora, was a ballet dancer. In the back of my mind, I felt if all else failed, if I couldn't remember a line, I could always pirouette away and I'd still be in character."

Her dancing ability had actually won Audrey the role. Andree Howard, an associate of Marie Rambert, had been hired to direct the ballet sequences in *The Secret People*, and she had lobbied all along for Audrey. But director Dickinson was put off by Audrey's inexperience and her nearly five-foot, eight-inch height. He thought she was too tall to play the younger sister.

"Up until *The Secret People*, somebody would want me for a minor role and I would take it or not," Audrey said. "With this movie began the long and protracted negotiations that I always thought were a complete waste of time. Of course, there are agents," she said. "What creative person, or any person for that matter, would want to spend time talking about the relative merits of height? The mechanics of film were much more mundane than dance, but the money was better."

Probably because she had been born into a wealthy family that had lost its fortune, money was always a practical concern of Audrey's, but she had none of the shame attached to it that people who crave it all their lives often exhibit. "A certain amount is a necessity," she said. "That amount changes with the times, of course, but anything over that is really unnecessary. I'm not just talking about enough for the bare essentials, either. Everyone develops a way to live, a style, that ultimately makes them feel comfortable, secure. For some it might mean Dubuffets and Dufys on the walls. I pity them, because that takes a fortune. For others, it may be roses in the garden and a machine that washes dishes. Without being greedy, which is a necessity for some sick people, everybody intuitively knows what they need. Desires are a different thing altogether. Money has nothing to do with them, but don't fall into the trap of confusing them with needs, either. But I did think this movie, and so many others, could help pay the bills."

The dance sequences in *The Secret People* proved extremely difficult for Audrey, and her always shaky self-confidence plummeted when director Dickinson informed her ally, choreographer Howard, that the fledgling actress was not up to snuff in the ballet either.

With her feet and ankles weak with exhaustion, Audrey continued to rehearse daily, never satisfying the perfectionist Dickinson, who was made even more curmudgeonly by a flu bug he just couldn't shake. By mid-March of 1951, the director was ready to film the ballet, no matter what. He rented a theater to serve as a backdrop for two days of nonstop work.

"The rooms were subarctic," Audrey recalled. "I always suffered from poor circulation [as is often the case with underweight people], but it was hard just to keep going when your fingers and toes are numb. The kids in the corps de ballet and I would do all kinds of experiments to gauge exactly how cold it was. A half glass of water left overnight would freeze solid. I wore three sets of leg warmers, and every time we had a break I'd warm myself by an electric heater. I was beginning to think acting was as torturous as hiding out in basements. And during the dress rehearsals, matters got worse. I had to take off the woollies and perform just in my tights."

Of course, physical discomfort was nothing new to her. After all, she had danced for hours while nearly starving to death during the German Occupation. This film, set at the time of the Resistance movement, forced her to confront awful memories and long-buried anguish. Yet it was this pain that brought a new dimension to her acting that was evident to everyone on the film.

In one of the most wrenching moments of

The Secret People, the sisters talk about a terrorist explosion. Audrey must describe the scene of death and dying.

"I couldn't do it," she recalled. "I thought I was going to have to give the money back and tell them I was sorry, but I couldn't talk about those things. It was as if the lines from the movie were about the real scenes I'd witnessed during the war. I had suppressed all that for a few years, and I realized now that it wasn't as if I were over it, I just ignored it. But all the images came back. I could do nothing to prevent them. Every time I tried to memorize the scene I became frozen."

Costar Valentina Cortesa did her best to give Audrey strength during the scene. She allowed her eyes to well up in empathy. When that didn't work, she developed a steely gaze. She knew Audrey was extremely insecure about getting so big a part, and she didn't want to feed into her doubts.

Director Dickinson advised her to concentrate on the horrific images that were passing before her eyes.

"I sat in a chair in a far corner of the set and watched all that went on in Arnhem as if it were a movie," Audrey recalled. "In fact, what took place was more devastating than the real movie they made about it [Richard Attenborough's 1977 war epic, *A Bridge Too*

110

Far]. And I was connected to it. Instead of blotting it out, I let it wash over me. I felt it. Then, since I didn't die like I thought I would, I used the emotion for the scene. That advice was better than any acting class I ever took before or since. It made me rely on the genuineness of my feelings. And it taught me all I know about concentrating."

When she delivered her monologue now, tears streamed down her face, and her costars felt they were witnessing an important moment. While the movie was not a commercial success, it had wide appeal in art houses, and it established Audrey as a serious actress. Ironically, only after she achieved that status was she offered the light, frothy roles which she made famous. It was as if the directors of those films needed reassurance that Audrey was serious in the hopes she'd lend dignity to their comedies.

In fact, on the strength of her performance in *The Secret People*, she was offered a minor part in the film *Monte Carlo Baby*, an inane diversion about a movie star involved in chasing after a missing baby. The movie starred Jules Munshin (best known for his role as one of the sailors in *On the Town*); Cara Williams, the comedienne who was about to marry John Barrymore, Jr.; and bandleader Ray Ventura, who also produced it, hoping to carve out an ancillary career for himself in film.

Audrey recalled with a laugh, "I took the part for my usual upstanding reasons: I was to play the part of the movie star and the costumes were fabulous. There was a Dior dress I was told I could keep. That was reason number one. Number two is that it was being filmed on the Riviera and I thought Mother could use a vacation. She had been feeling blue lately, possibly because I was seeing so much of James [Hanson]. Number three is the movie I really wanted, *Brandy for the Parson*, was postponed just enough for me to be practical and go with the one at hand."

But her visions of a leisurely shoot with plenty of time to explore beaches and cafés was ruined by the primary reasons she had been given the part: Hoping for wider distribution and more profits, Ventura wanted to film the movie in both French and English. Audrey would have to first deliver her lines in French, then in English. It was an interesting lesson in acting, to say the least.

More important, the rigorous shooting schedule kept her tied down to the Hotel de Paris, an opulent, overdone amalgam of marble and gilt which most days served as the location site.

In one scene, director Jean Boyer was trying to convince Audrey that she should smile and giggle more to lend the right feeling to her character, a young woman who was having a good time on her honeymoon.

Out of the corner of her eye, she noticed an elderly woman in a wheelchair, sternly giving directions to the man who was wheeling her around.

"All the time Monsieur Boyer was speaking to me, I was watching this older woman tell this slightly younger man what to do. And I thought, giggles are nice, but I bet this woman wouldn't smile a lot to show she was having a good time. She'd just keep on doing what she was doing. She had this bizarre red hair, all curls, and every time she'd make a point, her curls would bounce emphatically, too, like all these exclamation points shooting from her head. Her cheeks were painted red. I mean, they looked as if they'd literally been painted. As much as she was being pushed around by her husband, it was clear she was also pushing him around."

The overbearing woman was Colette, one of the most beloved modern novelists in France, a chronicler of the feminine heart in the *Claudine* books and the *Chéri* series. She and her husband, writer and editor Maurice Goudeket, were in Monte Carlo as guests of Prince Rainier of Monaco, as they had been during several previous winter seasons.

"When I realized who it was, I was overwhelmed," Audrey said. "I was always much more impressed with writers and artists than actors. I had read Colette's work as a young girl, and I always loved her simple style in conveying so much emotion. Here she was! It made me nervous to think she might be forced to watch me, since the lobby was closed off until the scene was shot."

But Colette didn't want to go anywhere. From the moment she set eyes on Audrey, watching her spritely movements, marveling at the wisdom in her young face, Colette was captivated.

She stayed for about an hour the first day, after director Boyer had at first been incensed that she was making noise. He turned to chastise her, but when he realized it was Colette, the Frenchman demurred. She was a national treasure. She could interrupt any movie she liked.

When she returned the next day just as shooting resumed, Boyer sighed, reconciled to the fact that another day might be lost to Colette's curious fascination with moviemaking. Her husband quietly assured the director that they had a singular purpose in watching the proceedings and that they certainly wouldn't stay long. "Madame finds the whole process enervating," he said.

Yet Goudeket pushed Colette closer to the center of action. Her wheelchair became entangled with the sound cables running the length and width of the terrazzo floor. She raised her gloved, birdlike hands to shield her eyes from the klieg lights, and dramatically pointed at Audrey.

"Voilà," she said. "That's my Gigi."

Gigi, Colette's 1945 novella about a young girl trained by her aunt to be a courtesan, was being adapted for Broadway. For two years, the production team had been searching for a leading lady. Talent scouts had been dispatched to comb Europe and America for a suitable actress to portray the coquettish child who develops into a warm, loving woman.

Audrey was unaware that she was being considered for the role by its creator, but she was nonetheless made extremely self-conscious by all the attention, especially since her lines in *Monte Carlo Baby* were so stupid. She was embarrassed to be saying them in front of an audience.

Goudeket pulled aside an assistant director and learned that Audrey would have to be approached through her mother. The formidable Baroness, seated away from the action in a corner armchair doing needlepoint, was pointed out. He approached her gingerly; she looked like an impenetrable gatekeeper.

He told her that Anita Loos, author of *Gentlemen Prefer Blondes*, had adapted *Gigi* for the stage almost as soon as it was published, and that she and producer Gilbert Miller had been searching since then for a suitable leading lady. There was serious talk of postponing the production indefinitely since no actress seemed to fit the requirements. Now his wife Colette was sure that Audrey would be the ideal candidate, and he had to agree. "I have never felt an actress was so emotionally right before," he told the Baroness. "She has this virginal seductiveness that marks Gigi. My wife is getting in touch with the producer right now."

Across the room, hunched even lower in her wheelchair, Colette painstakingly wrote a note to Loos that she had found Gigi and to alert Miller. At seventy-eight, her arthritis was so painful that she was unable to compose more than one note that day.

After shooting stopped that afternoon on *Monte Carlo Baby*, the Baroness quietly broke the wonderful news to her daughter.

"And I was petrified," Audrey said. "Looking back, I wasn't the least bit excited. I was just scared. I wished that they had never seen me, because I didn't want to go through the humiliation of showing them that I wasn't really an actress, that I couldn't sustain a leading

116

role on the stage. I remember speaking to James that night and he agreed that I couldn't do it. I remember thinking that he just wanted me to stay at home anyway, so his opinion couldn't really be trusted, but I myself knew that I couldn't do it.

"Mother and I had the loudest, longest argument of our lives that night. She, of course, was delighted at the turn of events. Not only would I go to New York and become a big star, in her opinion, but the scenario would eliminate James Hanson.

"Everybody seemed to have a secret agenda that day but me. I just wanted to finish the movie and go to the beach."

Because her mother literally forced her to meet with Colette, Audrey went to the writer's hotel suite and listened politely to her astounding proposal.

"I'm so sorry to waste your precious time, Madame," Audrey told Colette. "But what you don't know is that I cannot act. I could never play a leading role now, maybe not ever. I cannot be your Gigi."

Colette dismissed Audrey's objections with a fling of her gloved hand. She had done her homework, and was aware of Audrey's ballet and cabaret experience, although maybe not the limited extent of it. "You've worked hard all your life," Colette told her. "I have faith that all that work is about to pay off now," she said. "For both of us."

Audrey continued to decline the offer, with a steadfast vehemence that reminded Colette and her husband of Gigi's own adamant refusal to marry Gaston in her story. They watched the way her almond-shaped eyes grew even bigger and more lustrous as she said no. They saw the way she bounded about the hotel suite, dancer's toes pointed out, as she nervously explained her reasoning.

The more she refused, the more they had to have her.

Colette was optimistic that all Audrey needed was a little gentle persuasion and coddling. She advised Goudeket to send a cable to New York: "Don't cast your Gigi until you receive a letter from me."

Although neither Anita Loos nor Gilbert Miller put much stock in Colette's eye for talent, they did realize the importance of keeping the novelist happy. They agreed to interview Audrey that summer in London, hoping that in the meantime they'd find their Gigi among the ranks of genuine actresses.

Audrey, on the other hand, was finally coming around. "Colette did everything she could to bolster my confidence," she recalled. "I still have a photo that she gave me at the time. It's inscribed, 'To Audrey Hepburn, the treasure I found on the beach.' "

When she finally walked into producer Miller's suite at the Savoy Hotel in London, Audrey had let go of her fear. As much as she wanted the part, she was still troubled by the notion that it might mean her marriage to Hanson would be postponed. Yet since she hadn't seen much of him recently, she agreed that there was no hurry and that going to New York might be fun.

Miller was rather less enthusiastic. The veteran producer of important plays, including the debut of T. S. Eliot's *The Cocktail Party*, wondered if Audrey was strong enough both physically and mentally to carry a Broadway show on her frightened shoulders. An obese man, Miller was sure that Audrey had to be dreadfully ill to be so thin. But he was charmed by her international accent and dark, stunning eyes. He knew that if he didn't hire her, another producer would. Despite the fact that her experience was minimal, he decided he wanted her for the title role in *Gigi*.

As a matter of courtesy, he asked her to stop by Anita Loos's suite down the hall. When Audrey entered, Loos was catching up with her good friend Paulette Goddard. The actress didn't say a word as Loos kindly asked Audrey a few questions and attempted to make small talk to get to know her a little.

According to journalist Charles Higham, Goddard was unable to contain herself after Audrey left the room.

"There's got to be something wrong with that girl," Goddard reportedly said to Loos. "Anyone who looks like that should have been discovered before she was ten years old!"

At twenty-two, Audrey was on the verge of becoming a major star. Miller decided to give her a contract, despite the fact that she flubbed her lines and became extremely flustered and uncomfortable at the impromptu audition he held at a West End theater.

To make matters worse, veteran stage actress Cathleen Nesbitt was positioned at the back of the balcony to see if Audrey could project to the entire house. She had to report that she could hear absolutely nothing. Yet Miller had so much faith in Audrey's ability to capture an audience's complete attention that he used his expertise to help Audrey get out of her contract for additional films with Associated British Pictures. He began to believe that no other Gigi would do. Blind faith carried the day.

He made an astounding announcement to the press. He said he had hired to portray Gigi "a young actress whose two years' stage experience had been confined to dancing bits in topical revues, a young actress whom we have never seen on stage." This was too good a story to pass by. Journalists were then desperate to photograph and interview this amazing creature who had so captivated the veteran producer.

Naturally, Audrey was not altogether pleased by the attention.

"They wanted me to stand in so many different silly poses," she recalled. "I felt like a cow at the country fair. But Mother encouraged this nonsense. She was ahead of her time in that she knew the value of publicity long before most people did. It's funny: She was a very serious woman; my God, she had spent her time saving lives! And maybe because of that, she knew innately that entertainment was going to take on unbelievable importance. I guess she basically knew that life wasn't so much fun, that it was filled with heartache, and that getting away from your problems, being entertained, would become a major leisure-time activity. She loved the performing arts as much as I did. She instilled in me a deep love of culture. But when the three-ring circus of Broadway and movies came beckoning, she knew that's where the money was."

Yet the new pressures, however exciting, instilled a real sense of dread in Audrey. Children who lose a parent at a young age through death or divorce, as Audrey had, often have an overwhelming fear of abandonment and loss. When life was going well for Audrey, she would frequently anticipate the end of that happiness. She'd fret about it so much, in fact, that it became a self-fulfilling prophecy. Life had a way of complicating itself in spite of Audrey's best intentions.

That's precisely what happened after she was given the part of Gigi. Days later, emissaries of director William Wyler caught Audrey doing a public appearance to promote a face cream she was paid to advertise and quickly cabled their boss that she should be considered for his upcoming movie, *Roman Holiday*.

Once again, she was conflicted about the good fortune. "I worried that if I expressed too much interest in the movie, [*Gigi* producer] Gilbert Miller might change his mind about me for the play. I got the sense he wasn't completely confident that I could do the part, and I wasn't either. I figured he wanted my complete attention.

"Then I worried about how I could do the play if the movie had to be filmed. I had never had one starring role; now I was faced with having two at once.

"And of course I worried about James. To be honest, I wasn't really sure I still wanted to get married to him, but I certainly didn't want to get out of it, either! I just didn't want to tell him. I didn't want to make anybody unhappy."

The couple had long discussions about their future together. Audrey had a difficult time explaining why she wanted to do the Broadway show, and how she could even consider *Roman Holiday.*

"It was hard for me to make sense of it myself," she said. "It wasn't as if I craved the attention. I didn't. I never did. It wasn't as if I wanted to prove to myself I could act. Frankly, I never felt I really could be anything more than adequate. But I realized, at that time at least, that other people, directors and casting people, felt differently. They had faith in me. My mother had faith in me. She often talked about wasting my talents. I didn't want to waste a single thing. My attitude was, 'I should give this a try. Everybody else thinks it might be the thing for me to do.'

"It's interesting that the only person objecting was the man I was supposed to marry. I guess even subconsciously, as much as I wanted to go along with him on the surface of things, I had to face the fact that part of me wanted to try this exciting thing. It would be an adventure, it would mean financial reward, and I would be forced to come out of my shell a little. Plus, and this is hard to admit, I could use it to postpone the wedding."

Gilbert Miller suggested that Audrey take a leisurely sail from London to New York in order to learn her lines. The ship she chose made the journey in eighteen days.

She was twenty-two years old. Except for the month she had spent hiding from the Nazis, she had never before been alone. She didn't handle it well. She gorged herself on chocolates during the entire passage. When she arrived in New York, ready to begin rehearsals but petrified nonetheless, she was fifteen pounds heavier.

Chapter 10

Her arrival in New York went completely unnoticed, exactly the way Audrey always liked
it.

But press agents for *Gigi* who picked her
up at the pier immediately set out to rectify
that. They dropped her off at an unobtrusive
midtown hotel, the Blackstone, and instructed
her to change for a ball game. She had no
idea what that was. Thankfully, she was always a simple dresser, and when she was captured by photographers cheering at Yankee
Stadium for the last game of the World Series,
she at least looked the part.

Not so when she arrived the next day at
the *Gigi* production offices at Rockefeller Center. Gilbert Miller was already feeling some
misgivings about having hired an unknown,
and an inexperienced unknown at that, and
he had a tendency to be cruel when he was
feeling anxious. "Put a little meat on your
bones, eh?" he said, sizing her up. "Don't
forget, we hired you for your bones."

In fact, Audrey, at five feet, seven and a

half inches, looked wonderful at 116 pounds, better than she had looked in her entire life. Insecure as she was, however, she vowed to stop eating until she lost the weight.

"And in my mind, I decided to also lose a few extra pounds, as insurance," she said.

Although in remission for several years after the end of World War II, Audrey's anorexic tendencies were reignited during the grueling rehearsals for *Gigi*.

After some initial embarrassing attempts to deliver her lines with a modicum of ease and inflection, Audrey sensed her days were numbered. She could see in the eyes of her fellow cast members that she was painfully bad. What made matters worse was that she could also see how much they were rooting for her success. But it seemed hopeless.

Cathleen Nesbitt, who had been hired to portray Aunt Alicia, Gigi's mentor in the play, was also given the part-time task of coaching Audrey in diction and delivery.

Every day after stage rehearsals with Michael Evans, Josephine Brown, Bertha Belmore, Francis Compton, Doris Patson, and the rest of the mostly British cast, Audrey would take a forty-five-minute train ride for further instruction at Nesbitt's country home.

"She would run like a deer down the platform at the train station calling, 'Hello, Cathy dear, I'm here! Let's get started,' in the sweetest, softest voice I'd ever heard," Nesbitt recalled. "That was the trouble. She couldn't project. No matter what I tried, Audrey just didn't have it in her to amplify her voice."

After a week without improvement, producer Miller began to entertain the notion of firing Audrey. He put out feelers for possible replacements. At the same time, he decided to fly Audrey to Paris for extra tutorials with Raymond Rouleau, the Belgium-born actor-turned-director who would become Audrey's most important ally on the production.

"To my utter surprise, he spoke very little English," Audrey recalled. "We conversed in French. Now in French, I felt like a great actress, isn't that strange? The language gave me confidence. So while I was over there, I felt I was finally doing well. I thought to myself that all I needed was a good director."

That respite of self-confidence would not last long.

Once the director met with the whole cast in New York, it became clear to everyone that the language barrier would prove to be a major obstacle. Although everyone could speak French with varying degrees of competence, the process of rehearsing in one language and actually conversing in another was tedious and energy-sapping.

Audrey became bored at the pace. She made matters worse, however, by exaggerating the stage directions. If she were instructed to walk across the room, she'd hurriedly skip. If she were told to laugh, she'd become hysterical. Throughout her life, she exhibited a tendency to go overboard in trying to please people. In this instance, she had been told by producer Miller to act more animated. So she became a clown. In addition, she was lightheaded from barely eating. The combination made her appear on the edge, about to slip over into mania.

Kitty Miller, the producer's empathetic wife, sensed the insecurity raging within Audrey, and insisted on taking her to lunch. "She just let me be," Audrey recalled. "She touched my hand a lot from across the table. I have no memory of what she said, but I was able to eat a little bit of steak that day, and I felt enormously better. I had lost nearly twenty pounds in a very short time, and looking back, I guess I was starving myself as punishment for not being the best actress ever to grace the stage.

"But it's funny: After I ate a little, I felt less judgmental. From then on, I was able to concentrate on my lines and modulate them. My nervousness lifted. Once that happened, I was able to give it my best shot."

In Philadelphia, where *Gigi* opened in its

pre-Broadway tryout, Miller dreaded the reviews. He was sure the critics would pan Audrey and consequently kill his show.

But she astonished Miller, and herself. In the pivotal scene where she rejects the debonair Gaston, she was finally able to do so with authority rather than the whiny petulance she'd shown throughout rehearsals. It was as if the character Gigi had finally jelled with the actress Audrey to become a radiant entity.

Although the critics were lukewarm about the play, they generally concurred that Audrey was the acting find of the year. "She gives a wonderfully buoyant performance which establishes her as an actress of the first rank," wrote the distinguished Henry P. Murdoch of the *Philadelphia Inquirer*.

She went to New York feeling "buoyant" and renewed, ready to . . . well, if not conquer Broadway, at least face it with equanimity.

Back at the Blackstone Hotel, David Niven had taken the room next door to Audrey's while in town to open opposite Gloria Swanson in a play called *Nina*.

A week before *Gigi* opened, Audrey rushed into Niven's room when something crashed on her windowsill, then fell to the ground.

"He was newly married," Audrey recalled, "and his lovely wife Hjordis was in the room, and God knows what I was interrupting, but I was too petrified to care. It turned out that a poor guest of the hotel on a high floor had become so despondent, he jumped. Well, as sad as this story was, when we found out what really happened, that it was the sound of a body thumping, we couldn't stop laughing.

"It was awful. There we were, the three of us, gleefully whooping it up over somebody's dreadful misfortune. But David was worried about his opening night, I was scared to death about mine, and that awful suicide broke the ice. I knew after that night, nothing was going to be so bad. I was going to make it, no matter what."

Gigi opened in New York on November 24, 1951, which happened to be Cathleen Nesbitt's sixty-third birthday. And in the scene where Nesbitt, as Aunt Alicia, instructs Audrey in the fine art of cooking and eating a lobster and picking and choosing a man (pursuits that were not so different in writer Colette's view), Audrey was able to wish her costar and mentor a happy birthday by whispering in her ear, without breaking character.

"I knew then that I could do this thing called 'stage acting,' " Audrey said. "I was no longer paralyzed. I could be myself and an actress, too."

Although she forgot several lines in her last

scene, Audrey had already impressed the critics to the point where they didn't care about a few missed sentences. It was the feeling that counted. And Audrey conveyed the feeling.

"Audrey Hepburn is a young actress of charm, honesty and talent," raved Brooks Atkinson in the *New York Times*. "Miss Hepburn is as fresh and frisky as a puppy out of a tub," wrote Walter Kerr in the *New York Herald Tribune*, adding, "She brings a candid innocence and a tomboy intelligence to a part that might have gone sticky, and her performance comes like a breath of fresh air in a stifling season."

Audrey was literally an overnight sensation. Producer Miller was completely won over. At the Fulton Theater he advised the stagehands to change the marquee. Before opening night, it had read: "GIGI with Audrey Hepburn." Afterward, it said: "AUDREY HEPBURN in GIGI."

On that fateful opening night of *Gigi*, a star wasn't so much born as baptized.

Now she had a harder task ahead. Having been branded a celebrity, Audrey could no longer retreat into the cocoon of obscurity. Once the flashbulbs started popping, they never stopped.

Chapter 11

It would never let her down, even as she grew older and wrinkled. The camera loved Audrey like a best friend.

And after her difficult (if ultimately successful) introduction to the stage in *Gigi*, she returned to movies as if running home to Mother.

Eminent director William Wyler embraced her like a prodigal daughter. The overseer of Academy Award-winning films like *Mrs. Mittiver* and *The Best Years of Our Lives* had been trying to cast the leading role in *Roman Holiday* for several years, ever since director Frank Capra had passed on the sweet, escapist comedy.

Those in Hollywood who read the screenplay found it irresistible. Originally conceived by the blacklisted writer Dalton Trumbo, *Roman Holiday* never had a chance at being produced until Trumbo asked his colleague, Ian McLellan Hunter, to front for him to help get the movie off the ground. The story of a princess who momentarily ignores her royal duties for an adventurous romp with a street-smart reporter was a sweet variation on the Cinderella myth. It had settings and characters that would appeal to highbrows and lowbrows alike.

Yet finding an actress to portray Princess Anne, an impish young woman severely constrained by the duties of her position, was a daunting task. She had to be beautiful but innocent, alluring yet untouchable. After Wyler failed to come up with a suitable candidate (Elizabeth Taylor had been interested five years before, when she wanted to star opposite Cary Grant), Paramount Pictures hired Paul Stein as a test director to interview and film actresses in fifteen-minute audition pieces.

The studio was attempting to eke out advance publicity on *Roman Holiday*, and approached the search for Princess Anne much as David O. Selznick had the casting of Scarlett O'Hara in *Gone With the Wind*.

Audrey did her audition in London before she left for Broadway and the opening of *Gigi*. A small indication of her growing power is that she requested that Thorold Dickinson, her director on *The Secret People*, be allowed to film her for the test. Her wish was granted. Wyler had remembered her from a bit part in *Laughter in Paradise* and was smitten enough with her elegant beauty to capitulate to her wish.

"She completely looked the part of a princess," he said. "A real, live, bona fide princess. And when she opened her mouth, you were sure you'd found a princess. The one variable was: Could she act like a princess?"

At the time, Audrey wasn't sure she even wanted to continue acting at all; the more frightened she became, the more readily she found solace in the prospect of marrying James Hanson and settling down in Huddersfield as a dutiful wife.

Despite her reluctance, however, she was extremely impressive on the audition film, especially in the off-guard moments when she assumed the camera had stopped rolling. She was seated on a bed for the scene, and when Dickinson told her they were finished and she could get off of it, she winked.

"I didn't hear anybody say 'Cut,' " she said.

According to everybody who saw the audition film, Audrey won the role of Princess Anne in that brief moment, exuding charm and playfulness and a regal regard for propriety.

The test was flown to California and shown to Paramount executives, who, down to a one, fell in love with the impish Audrey.

"Exercise the option on this young lady," they wrote to their London representative.

"The test is certainly one of the best ever made in Hollywood, New York, or London. Hearty congratulations on behalf of Paramount." It was signed by Barney Balaban, Frank Y. Freeman, and Don Hartman, the studio's president, vice president, and production chief, respectively.

In that one short missive, Audrey was welcomed into the big time.

Designer Edith Head was dispatched at once to meet her and begin preliminary discussions about what a movie princess would wear. It was a smart move. Audrey salivated at the prospect of discussing clothing with anyone, let alone the preeminent Hollywood costumer.

She and Head quickly discovered they had similar tastes: simple lines, little ornamentation, superb materials. Audrey candidly discussed what she perceived as her physical shortcomings, and Head made copious notes about "scrawny arms, no breasts, and a neck that stretched on forever." But that was Audrey's assessment, not Head's.

The designer delighted in the possibility that she might be conceiving a wardrobe for this lithe creature, and immediately decided to incorporate Audrey's own schoolgirlish look — rounded collars and tailored suits — for the commoner side of Princess Anne. When Head showed her several sketches and samples of rich brocade to help clothe the character's regal persona, Audrey lamented her lack of curves.

"You should wear falsies," Head told her.

"What are they?" Audrey asked.

But she was not actually the shy little innocent in which the studio delighted. Executives at Paramount had hoped to turn Audrey into an indentured servant for seven years, the length of the contract they wanted her to sign. The feeling was that there always would be a role for Audrey in any movie, even if not a lead. With her splendid emaciation, she could play young or old, high fashion or virginal waif.

"She knew exactly how to highlight her good points," Head said. "What's funny is that her best look was as a sophisticated naif. What I liked best about her is that she calculated all her business decisions, but made it look as if she didn't have a clue."

Audrey steadfastly refused to sign the Paramount contract. Despite the fact that the studio tried to call her bluff and pretended it was going to give the role of Princess Anne to someone else, Audrey would not back down.

"I have Mother to thank for that maneuver," she said.

"Once I started to become popular, Mother

continuously tried to impress upon me that the ball was in my court, that I could call the shots. And since I really didn't care too much about whether I got the film or not, it did me no harm to follow her advice. After I listened to her for a while, I saw that she was right. The less accessible I was, the more people wanted me. I was never intentionally difficult, but I did decide up front what I required and I stuck by my guns.

"I remember when [*Gigi* producer] Gilbert Miller asked me to change my last name so that I wouldn't be confused with Katharine Hepburn. My name! I had no trouble getting rid of Edda, but Hepburn was my blood. I had to say no. In the end, I was respected for knowing what I wanted and not wavering."

Her personal life was another story. The more that agents and directors and producers sought her out, the more James Hanson became insecure about his status as her beau. He even went so far as to announce their wedding plans in the *London Sunday Times* without Audrey's permission.

He must have intuited that he was losing her. He began doing everything in his power to change the course of events. After it became clear that Audrey would be in America for the theatrical run of *Gigi* and the preproduction work on *Roman Holiday*, he moved the headquarters of his trucking business from England to Canada in order to be closer to his beloved.

Although they caught a few evenings together, Audrey's career took precedence over her personal life. Hanson began to sense that her devotion to him was faltering. He backed off for a time to see if she might begin to miss his attentions. But too much was going on in Audrey's life for her to regret any missed opportunities.

In May of 1952, Gilbert Miller disappointedly closed *Gigi* on Broadway, despite the fact that it was still selling out. Audrey's contract was up. She was scheduled to fly to Italy to begin work on *Roman Holiday*.

"The night we closed the play, I couldn't even join my colleagues in a little party," she recalled. "I had to hurry home and pack for Italy. I left the next day. It was too bad I couldn't say goodbye to the cast and crew. I was already working against my image as a snob because I didn't spend much time with the cast members, but that's because I was always taking lessons to improve myself.

"There were Wednesday afternoons where I would have loved to goof off with all of them between the matinee and evening performances, but I had to rush over to West Fifty-fourth Street for my dance classes."

She studied with a Russian émigré, Madama Olga Tarassova, whose teaching technique was far more rigorous than her predecessors' in Audrey's ballet career. But Tarassova's husband often hung around the studio, drinking and eating and generally interfering with the classes. Still, he was a welcome relief to Audrey.

"He was my entertainment for the week," she recalled. "I got a real kick out of his antics. He would drink a glass of vodka from the opposite side of the rim and spill nary a single drop in the process. He annoyed most of the other students, but I think I was secretly jealous of his freedom to do as he pleased. I didn't have that luxury. I wouldn't have it for years to come, and then when I finally could do exactly what I wanted, my desires remained pretty simple."

Like Princess Anne, Audrey's first major role and a part that would define her for the rest of her career, Audrey longed for simple fun and genuine friendship, desires often at odds with the realities of moviemaking.

By the time Audrey arrived in Rome in the summer of 1952 to begin filming the movie which would establish her as a film star of the first rank, the Hollywood publicity machine had already started rolling.

Paramount put her up at the four-star Excelsior Hotel. Cocktail parties were thrown in her honor. Strangers pretended to know her well. It was a whirl of high drama and artifice, where kisses polluted the air with empty promises.

At a welcoming party honoring Audrey and her famous costar, Gregory Peck, she got a small dose of the price of celebrity.

"I had never met Greg before that," she recalled, "and I was extremely excited. I mean, he was a movie star! It was inconceivable to me that we were in any way equals. But he was gentlemanly and gracious when we were introduced, certainly acting as if we were coming from the same place. He shook my hand with such strength that somehow I felt a little stronger. He hadn't said a word. I gave him a little peck on the cheek in gratitude."

That innocent kiss was enough to fan the flames of rumors everywhere.

Within days, newspapers reported the alleged affair between the stars of *Roman Holiday*. Paramount did nothing to quell the rumors. The studio was secretly delighted at the opportunity to promote the romance. It would be presented on the screen as an affair that had its roots in real life.

Any opportunity for "a little ink" was seized. *Roman Holiday* was released almost simultaneously with the announcement that England's Princess Margaret had fallen in love with a commoner, RAF Group Captain Peter Townsend. The coincidence between that fact and the plot of the movie was milked for all it was worth.

The actual making of the movie was prosaic in comparison to the stories swirling around it. The only real high drama had to do with the enervating heat in Rome that summer — 94 degrees outside, with temperatures reaching as high as 104 in the Palazzo Brancaccio, an eighteenth-century rococo palace where many of the early scenes were filmed.

"I can remember sweating more than I ever did even as a dancer," Audrey recalled. "For the scenes in my bedroom, I had to wear this pink woolen nightgown, very demure, covering me all up, and oh so hot! There were candle sconces on the walls, and the wax would melt in about an hour. The candles would have to be replaced. As I watched them drip between takes, I would lose strength, too. I identified with them. I think I felt as wilted as they did."

Despite director Wyler's insistence up until his death in 1981 that everything about the making of *Roman Holiday* was a delight, either his memory had faltered or he wished to mask the truth.

In fact, the tension on the set was palpable. Wyler was incensed with Paramount for insisting he film the movie in black and white. That was his "punishment" for wanting to film the entire movie on location in Rome. Yet once in Rome, he was not too happy about winning his demand and losing Technicolor. In addition, street fighting between Communists and Fascists often meant production had to be postponed.

In terms of personalities, although Gregory Peck was at the height of his popularity at the onset of *Roman Holiday*, at thirty-six he was already beginning to worry about maintaining his position. He wondered what having a complete unknown as his costar would do to his career. Wyler did nothing to build Peck's confidence, either; in fact, he neither praised nor chastised his actors, preferring instead to insist upon innumerable takes without acknowledging which one he would use.

With Audrey, however, the director was more solicitous. He coddled her, purring to her in his thick German accent that she looked fine on-screen.

At the time of shooting, Peck was making a last-ditch effort to save his marriage. He had invited his Finnish-born wife, Greta, and their three children to join him in a rented villa near Albano, twenty miles outside of Rome.

The effort soon fell apart and Greta and the kids left for Finland.

Audrey's personal life was coming to a boiling point as well. James Hanson had begun to read about the rumors linking Audrey and Peck, and he decided to press her on the marriage issue.

"Eventually, I had to call it off," Audrey said. "It became clear that I could not be the kind of wife James wanted, at least at that heady stage of my career when everything was moving so fast. I must say, I got caught up in the excitement. The movie actually began to seem more important than my impending nuptials, so I knew something was unmistakably wrong. Then the studio told me about my commitment to publicize the movie. They said that stuff was just as important as making the film. I felt I couldn't let them down, and I wasn't sure how long it would take to sell it."

But *Roman Holiday* needed little promotion when it was released in 1953. Even though it was her first major film performance, it was also one of Audrey's best, in part because she had a dual role: the real-life princess and the commoner she longed to be. Thanks to this twist on the Cinderella story, plus an engrossing combination of romance, comedy, drama, and an alluring Rome location, the movie appealed on many levels, despite its rather thin plot.

While making a European tour, Princess Anne (Audrey), the daughter of a king of an unnamed country, is completely constricted by her "handlers." She cannot enjoy herself for fear she is not behaving properly. The rules she must live by are stifling to this young woman who has a great urge to experience life. In the early scenes, you sense she is about to explode.

In an act of supreme rebellion for a member of the ruling class, she sneaks out of her royal boudoir one night to experience life on life's terms. But even her innocent little adventure is "controlled" — her maids have doctored her bedtime milk with a sleeping potion to prevent just such independence. But their overprotectiveness backfires. A drowsy, seemingly woozy Anne meets up with impoverished American journalist Joe Bradley (Gregory Peck). He kindly brings her back to his apartment to sleep it off.

In the morning, he realizes just who she is and quietly congratulates himself on his "find." She may be just the story he needs to boost a sagging career.

Bradley persuades his photographer friend Irving Radovich (Eddie Albert) to support the ruse financially by lending him enough money to take the princess on the town. The relationship between the two men is casual and teasing; Wyler does a wonderful job of differentiating between various kinds of friendship. The male bonding scenes have more energy and camera movement than the moments when Bradley and the Princess are alone. There is a quiet tentativeness to the composition, as if Wyler is building toward some revelation.

He delivers one the next day, when Princess Anne, free at last, savors the little things in life that seem mundane to the rest of us. She loves walking down the streets of Rome, unencumbered by her entourage. She delights in getting a haircut, kicking up her heels. The many beautiful sites astound her — she has never before been able to get so close to monuments she has read about. In fact, she is a kind of monument herself, except on this day when she comes to life.

But the fantasy of living an ordinary life must come to an end, as all fantasies do. While dancing with Bradley on a barge in the Tiber River, she is discovered by some of her minions. Although Bradley has by now fallen in love with her, Anne realizes that she must return to her world, the place she now feels she belongs.

At a press conference the next day, hordes

of reporters and photographers crowd the room where Princess Anne regally presides. When Bradley and Radovich approach her, she is polite, but vaguely unapproachable, telling the photographer she'll treasure the souvenirs he gives her (photos of her night and day on the town) while making idle small talk with Bradley.

Her one day among the people becomes more like a dream to the Princess, while her proletariat Prince Charming is left with nothing but the very real and painful memory of falling in love with a mirage.

Because *Roman Holiday* relies almost exclusively upon appearances to advance its plot, Audrey's "look" was vital to the success of the movie. Her bright-eyed magic illuminated every frame and immediately turned her into a star. It was an important distinction to note, and movie executives at every studio did. A virtually unknown actress had captivated audiences in a light, frothy entertainment that had more charm than substance.

Not only would Audrey's gamine pixie style change the definition of beauty in the next decade, her insouciant manner would encourage moviemakers to be more lighthearted. We would soon witness the buoyant age of American cinema, and Audrey would become its most elegant messenger.

Chapter 12

That exquisite blending of regal dignity and bubbly charm evident in *Roman Holiday* would carry Audrey through her next film as well, one that would have a profound effect on her personal life as well as her increasingly well-constructed image.

Sabrina, a bona fide Cinderella fairy tale, is the story of a lowly chauffeur's daughter who is transformed into a chic young woman after a European trip.

In Audrey's own life, she would meet the love of her life while making the movie. That relationship wouldn't last, but she would also meet another man involved with *Sabrina*, a designer, who would help Audrey create a signature look of severe simplicity that would define her style for the rest of her life and, sadly, outlast any love.

Audrey actually picked the property herself after reading Samuel Taylor's slight play *Sabrina Fair*, which was slated to be brought to Broadway with Margaret Sullavan in the lead. She asked her new agent, Lew Wasserman, then a relative newcomer to show business, to persuade Paramount to buy the property as a vehicle for her. After the surprising box office success of *Roman Holiday*, and Audrey's subsequent Oscar, Paramount was eager to please its new star.

In fact, she had made a brilliant choice for herself in terms of material, but would make a rather disastrous one when it came to personal interactions on the set.

Her costars, Humphrey Bogart and William Holden, would alternately come to hate Audrey and love her while working on *Sabrina*.

Falling in love with Holden was not something Audrey planned to do, nor was it something she ever talked about, but it was an incontrovertible fact, like her mink-brown eyes.

Those eyes, in fact, are what sparked the whole thing. The first time they met on the *Sabrina* set, their eyes locked and that was that. It didn't matter that Holden was married, the father of two sons. Something magical clicked between them, and a crowbar could not pry them apart.

"Audrey Hepburn's attractiveness radiates from her eyes," observed Australian actor John McCallum. "Sex certainly started in her eyes. And I think it's true generally, but we don't notice it because there are so few eyes like Audrey's. A close-up on film of an attractive woman's eyes is far sexier than a close-up of naked breasts. There is an expression to the effect that men make love to women's faces, and with Audrey, I'm sure it was true. I think Bill Holden was sunk from the moment he laid eyes on her. A goner, and all he did was look."

It would take some time for Audrey to realize that the man she was so smitten with was an argumentative alcoholic who would break her heart with a candid admission. And even after this became painfully clear to her, she would continue to love him.

Sabrina coscreenwriter Ernest Lehman remembered walking into Holden's trailer unannounced one day with some script changes when he realized something was going on.

"They were standing a foot apart," he recalled, "facing each other, their eyes meeting." He remembers being embarrassed, but not exactly sure why. "Something profound was happening between them," he said.

Known as a man's man, Holden was actually an insecure, neurotic bag of nerves underneath his bravura. His dual personality probably attracted Audrey — she herself remained insecure about her looks for her whole life, and was most comfortable with those people with whom she could share her doubts.

In any case, they were inseparable on the set of *Sabrina*, spending all their free time together. Audrey had a little green bicycle that had been given to her by Billy Wilder, *Sabrina*'s director, and she would ride it over to Holden's dressing room at the other end of the Paramount lot. Then they'd close the door.

In fact, once when Sidney Skolsky came to interview Audrey in her own dressing room (at one time the studio home of Dorothy Lamour), Audrey wasn't quite sure where anything was. She tried to offer the gentleman a drink, but didn't know if she had anything on hand to serve. The journalist found her arrogant. In fact, she was insecure.

But Skolsky was still impressed with her demeanor, despite the cliches he relied upon to tell his readers about Audrey. "You sit up and take notice," he wrote, "because her arrival is like a blare of trumpets. This is an actress in the grand manner: another Garbo, Bette Davis, Katie Hepburn, Greer Garson, Joan Crawford, or who-have-you. This is IT!"

That assessment was not shared by costar Humphrey Bogart. Probably out of jealousy over the fact that his love, Lauren Bacall, had been turned down for the title character of *Sabrina*, and coupled with the insecurity bred by binge drinking, Bogart resented the attention being heaped on Audrey.

"How do you like working with that dream girl?" Clifton Webb asked him one day on the Paramount lot.

"She's okay," he said ruefully, "if you like to do thirty-six takes." He deemed her an obsessive lightweight who continually tried to do better without much talent to go on.

And he didn't keep his opinion to himself, sharing his intense dislike of Audrey with all who would listen. People familiar with the facts assumed that Bogie was miserable himself.

He was actually a replacement for Cary Grant, who had had to pull out of *Sabrina* at the last minute. No amount of script tinkering save for a complete rewrite could make Bogart feel comfortable in the part of a debonair tycoon. But his character's personality really could not be revised to fit the more gruff Bogart if the plot of the movie were to advance as written.

Like *Roman Holiday*, *Sabrina* relies upon the believability of its central character undergoing a complete change. In this case, the time-honored traditional plot line of an ugly duckling turning into a swan was enhanced by an emotional transformation that paralleled the physical change. Audrey based her career on portraying just such characters — impish waifs who become the epitome of elegance before the final credits.

Edith Head, who was hired again to work with Audrey, almost quit the picture when she was told that she would only be working on costumes Sabrina would wear before her trip to Paris. A leading young designer, Hubert de Givenchy, would be given the task of creating Sabrina's sophisticated post-European wardrobe.

Audrey met with Givenchy in Paris in 1953. He was twenty-six, just two years older than she, and they immediately fell in love with each other's sense of style. She would become his muse; he would become her staunchest supporter and creator of the minimal look which defined her appearance. "Audrey knew herself perfectly," he said, "the qualities as well as the flaws. I think that's why she was so loyal to me. I didn't hide anything of hers. I let her be. But it just so happened, I didn't really believe she had many flaws in her appearance — and certainly not in her personality. But I humored her. In that first movie, she was terribly insecure about her bust line. But I told her people would look at her eyes first no matter what size her breasts were. Her eyes were that important. And I believed that. And I think I persuaded her of that, too."

Billy Wilder, the brilliant Austrian director

of such tough movies as *The Lost Weekend*, *Stalag 17*, and *Double Indemnity*, tackled the comedy of *Sabrina* with the same kind of intensity. He strengthened the humor by tailoring his screenplay (cowritten with Samuel Taylor and Ernest Lehman) to the female perspective. And unlike the many movies about the coming of age of young men, *Sabrina* makes clear that the process of sophistication a young woman endures is not because money or success is the anticipated reward. For a young woman's coming of age, romance is the payoff.

Sabrina wants to better herself and her situation because she has fallen in love with someone in a higher social order. It's simple, and certainly a more romantic story line than the usually more prosaic accounts written from the male perspective.

The plot is ingeniously simple: Sabrina Fairchild (Audrey), daughter of the Larrabee family chauffeur on Long Island, has aspirations above her station. As part of her grand ambition, she develops a crush on David Larrabee (William Holden), the younger Larrabee son. A quintessential playboy, he is disdainful of her attentions, deeming her a mere girl, not at all like the women he has been attracted to in the past, three of whom he married.

Because she is nearly invisible as the daughter of the chauffeur, Sabrina is able to spy on young Larrabee with unabashed nosiness. Wilder makes a great point of showing just how easily the ruling class ignores its underlings, and his documentary-style camera angles in these scenes — in which Sabrina is clearly in the frame but David Larrabee doesn't see her — points out the sad inequity of class without seeming polemical.

In one such moment, she watches David as he woos a young woman one evening on the family tennis court. Sabrina is so distraught over the hurtful reality that her attraction is not mutual that she attempts suicide by carbon monoxide poisoning in her father's garage.

But David's older brother, Linus (Humphrey Bogart), saves her.

Her father (John Williams) has begun to recognize that his daughter's fantasy life is encroaching upon his territory. He decides to send her away. Paris is chosen, not for its image as the City of Light or a center for lovers, but because it has some of the best cooking schools in the world. The chauffeur naturally expects his daughter to become a cook.

Sabrina turns out to be a hopeless cook, a stroke of great fortune for the rest of the movie, an inevitability, much like the wonderful luck that follows. An aging baron (Marcel Dalio) takes a benign interest in changing her image and begins to educate Sabrina in the ways of the cultured, wealthy, European aristocracy of which he is a leading member.

The make-over is complete. In an unabashed tribute to *Pygmalion*, when Sabrina returns to Long Island a poised and elegant young lady, David drives by the train station where she is patiently waiting for her father — and doesn't recognize her.

In one of the most enticing scenes of the movie, he gamely offers to drive her home — an obvious attempt at a pickup. Wilder highlights David's by now tired lines of seduction, while contrasting Sabrina's refined style and accomplishment in the art of conversation. Not until he pulls up in front of the family's palatial estate does he realize who Sabrina is.

The tables are turned; in fact, David is now so taken with Sabrina, it is as if there had been no tables before this. She is demure now, noncommittal, as he attempts to interest her in seeing him again.

Just as she is about to capitulate, older brother Linus — Sabrina's lifesaver — reappears and makes his intentions known. On the surface, he is the perfect suitor: wise, a trifle dull, but oh so reliable.

Curiously, Wilder interferes with the natural course of events here and introduces a plot twist that seems jarring and, ultimately, unsatisfying.

As a guest of David's at a party at the Larrabee mansion, certainly still "the big house" in Sabrina's eyes, she charms all the guests — most especially the gentlemen — with her quiet wit and undivided attention.

But David makes clear he doesn't want to share his "find," an unusual set of circumstances for the normally happy-go-lucky playboy. This change does not go unnoticed by Linus, who hovers around the party, always on the periphery, silently and quietly — almost sneakily — trying to arrange things in his own grand plan.

And he has one for brother David. In order to increase the family's holdings, Linus has arranged for David to marry a sugar heiress. He feels no remorse in pushing this outcome; after all, his brother has never exhibited a long attention span, never — current infatuation included — seemed truly in love.

But in order to effect these results, Linus decides he must make a play for Sabrina himself, to distract her from his more flamboyant brother. He is banking on the fact that his well-known reputation as a trustworthy fellow will now begin to appeal to the newly sophisticated Sabrina.

Linus plays the part well.

Sabrina slowly becomes smitten, and his stodginess begins to seem appealing after the rather unreliable David. Yet Linus has no plans other than aggrandizing the family business. He pretends to want to marry Sabrina only to concoct an elaborate plan to get her out of the country. On the pretext of a honeymoon trip, he tells her he's booked passage on a ship bound for Europe; in reality, he doesn't show up and she sails alone.

In yet another bit of outlandish change of heart, brother David, suddenly the good guy, lectures Linus about the importance of love. Apparently the heart-to-heart talk makes a difference, for Linus soon helicopters out to meet Sabrina midocean.

Ultimately, the audience is asked to swallow too many personality changes in one movie — with the exception of Sabrina's father, who gladly accepts his lot in life, the major characters in *Sabrina* all become completely different personalities by the end of the film. Of course, that was Audrey's stock-in-trade in the movies, but as *Sabrina* would prove, it was best if Audrey was the only character to undergo a transformation.

That's because when she was in a movie, audiences only paid attention to her. The other characters worked best when they were used as foils to her personality.

In the supremely confident and giving style that is one of his greatest strengths and defining characteristics, Gregory Peck recalled the moment when he realized Audrey was a star and he decided he had to do something about their billing.

"I was slated to get top billing on *Roman Holiday*, and despite the fact that Audrey's part was much larger, I didn't have any trouble getting more attention than she," he said. "It's not like I'm benevolent to an excessive degree. I would have retained the top billing, if I didn't realize without a doubt that Audrey would become a giant star after *Roman Holiday* and that if I didn't kindly cede to her my position in the credits, I would begin to look like an aging star desperately trying to hang on to status for security's sake.

"It was I who suggested that Audrey's name be prominently displayed in the advertisements. And I never regretted it. It made me seem prescient. But once you saw that sweet little girl in action, you knew you were dealing with a volcano of talent. Anybody who worked with her saw that."

And anybody who knew her personally learned that Audrey was also always on the verge of erupting emotionally. Her passion for Holden was disrupting her life. Because of the clandestine nature of their affair, Audrey was even more excited by their relationship. She wasn't eating or sleeping. She spent all her time thinking about him, and the stolen moments they spent together in his dressing room.

During the filming of *Sabrina*, Audrey often spent isolated weekends at home in her garden apartment while she obsessed about what her lover was doing at home with his wife and kids.

She lived in a modest two rooms on Los Angeles's Wilshire Boulevard, to which she would retreat on Friday after filming, refusing all invitations to go to dinner.

"I need to refuel," she would tell her prospective hosts. In fact, she would replay conversations with Holden, trying to deduce whether or not he was ready to leave his wife for her. She did not want to confront him until she was sure of the answer.

Once Audrey was convinced that Holden really loved her and wanted to marry her, she decided to postpone actually asking him to make a commitment, so sure was she that they were meant to be. Never had she felt so compatible with anyone on every level: intellectual, emotional, sexual.

Their obvious — and unannounced — love for one another seemed to anger Bogart even more. Already insecure about his abilities in the role, he felt further ostracized by their partnership. He became so hateful toward them that director Wilder unofficially banned him from socializing with the cast and crew after hours.

It was on one of those evenings that Audrey admitted to Holden that she wanted to spend the rest of her life with him. He told her that he had always loved her, from the first moment he laid eyes on her.

She worried aloud that his wife, Ardis (whose stage name was Brenda Marshall), would never get over his leaving her and starting a new family.

"But I can't start a new family," Holden told Audrey. "I've had a vasectomy."

In 1953, vasectomies were irreversible. Audrey wanted a family. Her desire for bearing children was so strong, so incontrovertible, that it made her decision a very simple, although extremely painful, one. She broke it off with Holden, ending the relationship with the love of her life. As vulnerable as Audrey seemed, she was steely and determined when it came to going after what she wanted. Or running away from what she didn't.

Audrey's performance in *Monte Carlo Baby* may have been forgettable, but the film gave her the chance to be seen by Colette, and be chosen for the part of *Gigi*. (UPI/Bettmann)

Pupil and mentor — Audrey Hepburn and Colette. (UPI/Bettmann)

Audrey with her then-fiancé James Hanson. Her rapid rise to stardom would leave their marriage plans behind.
(UPI/Bettmann)

Audrey with her husband, Dr. Andrea Dotti, in 1969.
(UPI/Bettmann)

With Gary Cooper in *Love in the Afternoon.*

In *Funny Face* Audrey put a bohemian spin on her gamin image.

In *Roman Holiday*
Audrey's blend of
innocence and
sophistication
charmed audiences
everywhere and
earned her an
Academy Award.

Mel and Audrey
with "Mr. Famous."

Audrey with Sean Ferrar, aged seven months. Motherhood was her greatest joy. (UPI/Bettmann)

With James Garner and Shirley MacLaine in *The Children's Hour*.

My Fair Lady proved to be one of Audrey's most exasperating film experiences.

Working with Albert Finney in *Two For the Road* had a liberating effect on Audrey.

Ralph Lauren, Billy Wilder, and Gregory Peck
salute Audrey as she is honored by the Film Society
at Lincoln Center on April 22, 1991.
(Ron Galella)

Audrey presents Sean Connery with the
American Cinematheque Award in July 1992, only
six months before her death. (UPI/Bettmann)

As someone who knew starvation as a child, Audrey Hepburn put her heart and soul into her work on behalf of UNICEF. (UPI/Bettmann)

Chapter 13

It was a typical rebound affair. Still smarting from the end of her relationship with Holden, Audrey was extremely vulnerable to love and attention when she met actor/director Mel Ferrer at a party in London.

Gregory Peck was the host, and he introduced the couple, thinking their European backgrounds might offer a common ground for an evening of talk.

"I never dreamed they would marry, though," Peck said.

Ferrer was filming *Knights of the Round Table* at the time, and he always was at his most charming when he was working.

"We talked about theater," Audrey recalled. "I had seen a few productions at the La Jolla Playhouse, and Mel had directed one of them, I think, and he was eager to talk about the craft of the stage. I loved it! Mel could make theater feel important, as important as the ballet. He was the first man to make me feel my profession was a worthy one. In retrospect, that was very important. Once it became clear I was going to work pretty steadily, it was great to feel good about what I was doing."

They monopolized one another at the party. By the end of the evening, Audrey begged Ferrer to send her any play he thought they might be able to do together.

Hollywood Reporter columnist Radie Harris, a longtime friend of Audrey's, recalled their attraction as "completely mutual. Is it any wonder that Mel Ferrer fell head over heels in love with such a provocative, desirable creature?" she asked. "Mel had always been attracted to glamorous, successful women. But the chemistry worked both ways. I can also understand why Audrey succumbed to Mel's charm.

"Mel has that rare quality in an American male: He makes a woman feel like a woman."

But with Audrey, that also meant making her feel insecure. As with many couples who fall in love, Audrey and Ferrer soon discovered each other's vulnerabilities. Ferrer often exaggerated Audrey's failures in coping in order to boost his own flagging self-esteem. Because Audrey enjoyed being taken care of, the imbalance of power in the early stages of their relationship suited each of them well.

Paradoxically, however, as Audrey's star continued to rise, she became more and more unsure about her abilities.

"Everything I did at a certain stage turned to gold," she recalled. "It was most unsettling. I remember thinking it was a big mistake when I was nominated for an Oscar for *Roman Holiday*, but then when I was nominated again for *Sabrina*, I felt somebody was playing a cruel joke. I wasn't so good in that one, and I wondered how come nobody else noticed. Well, nobody except Mel. It's not that he criticized me, but he assessed my performance in a very professional way. He was my anchor to reality."

On September 7, 1953, soon after *Roman Holiday* had become an international hit, *Time* magazine featured Audrey on its cover, a momentous occurrence for a screen newcomer. In the article about her, *Time* wrote: "Audrey Hepburn gives the popular old romantic nonsense a reality which it seldom had before. Amid the rhinestone glitter of *Roman Holiday*'s make-believe, Paramount's new star sparkles and glows with the fire of a finely cut diamond. Impertinence, hauteur, sudden repentance, happiness, rebellion, and fatigue supplant each other with speed on her mobile, adolescent face."

Perhaps the great irony was that while Audrey was being crowned as Hollywood royalty, she was not a product of Hollywood at all. As a girl she had immersed herself in dance, in theater, in music and books. She studied languages, not movie magazines. She survived a war, not lines at the Bijou to see Betty Grable. She who had never been interested in the glitter and the glamour was suddenly taking Hollywood by storm.

The attention unnerved Audrey. What bothered her even more were the glowing comments of people who knew her. Her *Roman Holiday* director William Wyler concluded that "Audrey might be too good for some people," as he told one reporter who was doing a story about the girl who seemed as comfortable in an evening gown as in a pair of jeans.

"After so many drive-in waitresses in movies — it has been a real drought — here is class," Wilder went on. "Somebody who went to school, can spell and possibly play the piano. She's a wispy little thing, but you're really in the presence of somebody when you see that girl. Not since Garbo has there been anything like her, with the possible exception of Ingrid Bergman."

Bergman herself was taken with Audrey's debut. After seeing *Roman Holiday* in Italy, she came out of the theater dabbing her eyes. "What are you crying for?" her husband, Roberto Rossellini, asked her. "I was so touched by Audrey Hepburn," said the star of *Casablanca*, "that I had a genuinely emotional response to her performance."

As more and more people, both celebrities and commoners, began to appreciate Audrey's appeal, the men in her life were becoming frustrated by her inaccessibility.

Holden still tried to woo her, not realizing his inability to father any more children killed any possibility of a union between them. When she made it perfectly clear that she didn't want to see him at all, he took his disappointment around the world, courting a different woman every night.

Ferrer, on the other hand, realized how much Audrey cared about him, but recognized they had to be in the same country on the same coast for the relationship to test itself.

He had a plan. He sent her a copy of a romantic fantasy, Jean Giraudoux's *Ondine*, that he thought she'd be perfect in. He didn't spell it out, but implicit in his suggestion was the idea they'd costar in the play.

Ferrer was a savvy negotiator. Unbeknownst to Audrey, he had secured the services of the famed Alfred Lunt as director by promising him that Audrey would star in *Ondine*. Part of the package was that Ferrer would also have a role.

Despite his obvious talents and successes,

Ferrer had a difficult time working steadily as an actor. At thirty-five, he was still in wonderful physical shape, his frame still lean and muscular thanks to a regimen of tennis and fencing. But his rough good looks were not matinee-idol perfect, and many roles that he might have portrayed with ease were not given to him.

His personality, too, was different from the norm for actors. Ferrer was extremely intelligent and occasionally argumentative. Fluent in French, articulate, worldly, and opinionated, he was often mistaken for a diplomat in the international circles in which he traveled. A Princeton dropout, son of a Cuban-born Manhattan surgeon and his Irish-American heiress wife, Ferrer was born in Elberon, New Jersey on August 25, 1917. He turned to acting when he realized he was too restless to devote himself to studying.

When that career didn't pan out quickly enough, he began writing angst-ridden fiction. When that pursuit, too, seemed to be developing too slowly, he wrote a children's book, *Tito's Hat*, that was well received. But the effort hadn't challenged him enough. A short stint in summer stock led to a job as a dancer on Broadway. He was finally beginning to feel at home among the glamour and hard work of the stage.

But a bout with polio had shriveled his right arm, and while Ferrer worked unstintingly at getting back full usage, he learned one of the most important lessons of his life: Patience and discipline can get you through the toughest times. He left for Hollywood soon after and achieved minor success as a director of screen tests for David O. Selznick. Of course, he still wanted to be an actor, but he was willing to postpone his dream with more realistic expectations.

Yet by the time he met Audrey, he had costarred as a black physician who passes for white in *Lost Boundaries*, a lame puppeteer in *Lili*, and a toreador in *The Brave Bulls*. He had also been married three times: twice to sculptress Frances Pilchard (with whom he had a son and daughter) and once to homemaker Barbara Tripp (with whom he had another son and daughter).

In the beginning of their budding relationship, Audrey was extremely businesslike, knowing that a strong emotional entanglement could muck up the work they had to do to prepare *Ondine* for Broadway. But she couldn't hide her feelings for too long. "I saw him, liked him, loved him. It was as simple as that," she said about her attraction to Ferrer.

But Alfred Lunt, the revered actor and director who was hired to oversee *Ondine*, would not find it so simple. According to his equally revered wife, Lynn Fontanne, Ferrer used Audrey's crush on him to rule her with an iron fist. And in the process, he nearly ruined *Ondine*.

Audrey's supreme loyalty to those she loved was always apparent, but in the first flush of romance with Ferrer, she would listen to no one else.

The Russian-born couturier Valentina, who had been hired by Lunt to do the fantastical costumes for *Ondine*, told her husband, George Schlee (onetime business manager for Greta Garbo), that Audrey refused to make an even minor decision on outfits for the show without consulting Ferrer.

Schlee told columnist Radie Harris that Ferrer was a "veritable Svengali, exercising influence in every area of Audrey's life, from the food she ate [or didn't eat] to the number of sentences she spoke to reporters. It was as if," Schlee said, "he couldn't get a handle on his own life or career, so he decided to fixate on Audrey's."

In the opulent town house on East Sixty-seventh Street that also served as Valentina's business offices, Audrey would arrive each morning for her fittings. With her tiny body and minuscule measurements — 34" – 20" –

34" — the designer had to be extremely careful at striking a balance between beauty and whimsy. She could not overwhelm her charge with too much detail of design, nor could she be so simple that Audrey might look like a waif rather than a nymph.

According to Schlee, Audrey second-guessed every one of Valentina's ideas, making sure in her mind that Ferrer would approve of the choices being made.

Valentina, an extremely tall, extremely dramatic woman who counted among her clients the Duchess of Windsor, Paulette Goddard, and Queen Marie of Romania, was not used to discussing her creations before executing them. In her beautiful fitting room, dominated by an eighteenth-century chandelier, a life-size mannequin served as the initial model for Valentina's ideas. But with Audrey, who was so much smaller than the mannequin, Valentina had to drape Audrey herself to get a notion of what would suit her as the title character in the Giraudoux play.

The fantasy centered on the relationship between the knight-errant (Ferrer) and the water sprite Ondine, and Audrey wanted her costumes to suggest the otherworldliness of her character. In fact, it was Ferrer who first described to Audrey what he thought would be suitable attire: layer upon diaphanous layer of pale chiffon and netting knotted with tiny shells.

While Audrey stood, often for hours at a time, Valentina talked animatedly of giving men the illusion of having the upper hand, while actually retaining it for oneself. But Audrey was concerned that the layers of her costumes not become too thick. Ferrer had stressed to her that sheer limpidity was the look she should aim for.

At the 46th Street Theater, where Audrey rehearsed relentlessly with Ferrer and the rest of the cast, the mood was considerably more tense. *Roman Holiday* had magnified Audrey's star and made it shine even brighter, while the more modest success of *Lili* had done little for Ferrer's reputation. Everybody from lighting experts to sound technicians wanted to be introduced to Audrey, but nobody much cared about Ferrer. His already fragile ego could not withstand many more hits.

But they came. Alfred Lunt, the epitome of an English gentleman, was also a director, and in that capacity he was required to tell his cast members what to do. According to wife Lynn Fontanne, whenever he gave direction to Audrey, she would look to Ferrer to get the final okay. Not only did it infuriate Lunt, it slowed down rehearsals and alienated Audrey from the rest of the cast and crew.

But still she was devoted to putting on the best show she could. On the evening *Ondine* opened in Boston in its pre-Broadway run, her agent sent word that the first preview of *Sabrina* in California had drawn raves from the audience. When Ferrer congratulated her on the news after the first act, she was nonplused for several minutes. "That's all very nice and very fine," she finally said. "But don't you think the first act ran rather long and too slowly?"

Ferrer agreed that it was too long, and he took it upon himself to mark some dialogue he thought could be cut and show it to director Lunt. Lunt had not bargained on having a codirector on *Ondine,* and he bridled at Ferrer's interference. But when it came time for curtain calls every evening, there was Ferrer at Audrey's side. She insisted he share the limelight with her. Although audiences were aghast that he took his bows with her, Ferrer wanted to bask in Audrey's acclaim. It felt good. He had never received such an outpouring of warmth for any of his performances.

When the play opened in New York on February 19, 1954, all kinks had been ironed out. But the stress had wreaked havoc on Audrey's health. She had lost ten pounds since rehearsals began and had developed such a bad cold, she feared she would have no voice to recite her lines. But the same willpower that had seen her through the devastation of war guided her through the paces of her official opening night.

It was all a blur to her. "I don't remember getting onstage or saying my bits or even the final curtain call," she said. "All I can picture is the tons upon tons of floral arrangements packed into my dressing room when I returned. It was beautiful really, a garden in New York. I luxuriated in those flowers."

The drama critics threw bouquets as well. While Audrey and Ferrer and her mother attended a party in her honor at the French Embassy, Brooks Atkinson of the *New York Times* rhapsodized about Audrey in his office. "She is tremulously lovely," he wrote. "She gives a pulsing performance that is all grace and enchantment, disciplined by an instinct for the realities of the stage."

He described the production as "ideal from every point of view. Ideal literature, ideal acting, ideal theater — it hardly matters how you approach it. We are lucky. There's a magical play in town.

"Everyone knows that Audrey Hepburn is an exquisite young lady, and no one has ever doubted her talent for acting. But the part of Ondine is a complicated one. It is compounded of intangibles — of moods and impressions, mischief and tragedy. See how Miss Hepburn is able to translate them into the language of the theater without artfulness or precociousness."

There was no doubt about it: Audrey had been embraced by one of the toughest theater critics around. Yet she was curiously unfazed by the praise. Asked soon after opening in *Ondine* for her definition of success, she said, "It's like reaching an important birthday and finding out you're exactly the same. All I feel is the responsibility to live up to it. And even, with luck, survive it."

Her personal definition of success would not change. Throughout her life, Audrey looked upon accomplishments as responsibilities which complicated her life. There was the momentary thrill, and then a return to hard work. She really didn't know how to relax, until it was too late and she had gotten herself sick with exhaustion.

A month after she had won the Tony for *Ondine* and the Oscar for *Roman Holiday*, Audrey was on the verge of a nervous breakdown. Yet she never missed a performance of *Ondine*. Every evening, after being feted with multiple standing ovations, she left the 46th Street Theater and rushed to her apartment. Her mother and a doctor would try to force-feed her, at least making sure that she drank enough water to prevent dehydration. The effects of success, celebrity, her love for Ferrer, and her mother's hatred of him combined to nearly push her over the brink. Her inability to eat had caused malnourishment, and now she was suffering from anemia.

Gossip columnists everywhere were busy trying to scoop one another with announcements of Audrey's imminent engagement to Ferrer, but her mother kept them just as busy with her demands for retractions. The Baroness was adamant in her refusal to accept the thrice-married Ferrer as a suitable suitor for her daughter, and she and Ferrer engaged in an awful push-and-pull with Audrey, the woman they both reputedly loved. Audrey suffered mightily.

"I loved my mother with one-half of my heart," she said. "And I loved Mel with the other half. There was no room for compromise. It ate away at me that they couldn't get along."

The doctor who had been treating Audrey advised that she take a long rest cure. He was worried about both her physical and emotional well-being. Headlines bannered the news: "Audrey Hepburn Ill" and "Audrey Hepburn Rests Between Shows." In May, her doctor ordered her to leave *Ondine*. She worried about disappointing the play's producers, and worried more about having to immediately fulfill obligations at Paramount, which had kindly granted her a sabbatical on her contract.

But then she became too sick to worry. Although she had tried for months to please everybody she encountered, it was finally time to think of herself.

The producers of *Ondine*, fooled by the fact that she had not missed a single performance in the show's run, tried to persuade her to stick with it through the summer. Then Associated British Pictures chief Robert Clark arrived in New York with two movie scripts, one by the esteemed novelist Graham Greene, for Audrey to consider to fulfill her obligations to the Elstree Studios in London, the place that had launched her career.

In late June of 1954, Paramount offered to buy her out of her Associated British obligations for $1 million, the highest figure to that date ever bid on a foreign movie star. Ironically, just as she was beginning to command a megastar salary for the day, like the $2,500 a week she was paid on Broadway (plus a percentage of the profits) for *Ondine*, Audrey had to drop out of the scene for health reasons. Sadly, after she returned from Europe, she could never quite recapture the financial footing she had achieved before she left.

"Money never made anyone happy in and of itself," she said. "But it always gave me a real sense of security, so it enhanced my ability to be happy. But I always worked with what I had, hiding away my acorns just like the squirrels. Sometimes there were more acorns, sometimes less. But I was never without at least one nut!"

Chapter 14

What Audrey publicly called "the agony of recharging the battery" was in effect a medically mandated period of rest and recuperation necessary, in the view of her doctors, to prevent a complete nervous breakdown.

In Switzerland, where she went in late summer 1954 to escape the penetrating gaze of a public hungry for anything to do with one of the world's most popular stars, she was ordered to stay in bed.

The pain of facing herself was almost worse than the physical and mental anguish that had brought her to this point. "Here I was, newly crowned a big star, applauded for giving pleasure to so many people, and I finally woke up to the fact that I didn't know how to please *myself*. I was gravely unhappy, miserable really. I guess they would call it now a severe depression. I should have been on top of the world — in fact, high on the mountains in Burgenstock I *was* — but my morale was shot.

"I began to question everything: my love for my mother, for Mel. I began to wonder why I took up acting in the first place. It seemed I had spent my whole life trying to please other people, without having a clue as to what I wanted. Lying there on those plump pillows, I realized I had a lot to figure out."

One area in which she felt completely out of control was her lack of appetite. Although it appears obvious in our disease-obsessed era that Audrey suffered from a form of anorexia nervosa, during the 1950s eating disorders were not often diagnosed.

But the nonexistence of a desire to eat was characteristic of anorexia, a multidetermined and relentless drive to thinness. The psychological and endocrinological disease centers on denial — of hunger, thinness, and fatigue — and Audrey certainly exhibited these tendencies at various stages of her life. In Switzerland, forced to endure complete bed rest, she had at least begun to accept the fact that something was wrong with her.

Before she got to the secluded haven of Burgenstock, a serene mountaintop overlooking Lake of Lucerne, Audrey made the mistake of choosing the trendy Palace Hotel in Gstaad, the sophisticated enclave of winter sports.

"Somebody got the bright idea that because I was a movie star, I would need to be surrounded by flashy types, even if I was confined to my bedroom," Audrey recalled. "That's why Gstaad was recommended. And some other misguided sorts plastered the town with posters from *Roman Holiday* and started a rumor that I was going to attend a fancy dinner in my honor.

"Dinner? I could barely keep down a little soup. Plus, I developed a kind of asthma, which made my breathing labored, so there was absolutely no way I could even talk to anyone, let alone give a little speech. I was in a bad way on every front, and I left Gstaad after a miserable week."

But in Burgenstock, perched atop Lake of Lucerne, the healing powers of fresh air and serene scenery began to work their magic on this pathetically skinny creature.

At the Villa Bethiana, the small chalet Audrey rented primarily because it had wonderful heating, she soon began to rally outdoors in the sunshine, finally eating enough to be able to play a few sets of tennis and a few rounds of golf. Here enthusiasm for living gradually returned with her appetite, and soon she was counting the days until she could see her "beloved Mel" again. It rained a lot while she was waiting, and the weather seemed to cleanse her of any lingering doubts she had about the viability of her love for him.

Ferrer was nearby in Italy, filming *Le Madre*

in Rome, uncertain about what the outcome of his separation from Audrey would be. On his thirty-seventh birthday in August, however, Audrey made clear that she still wanted him, despite the physical and emotional pain he had caused by trying to control her life. She sent him a platinum watch to honor the occasion, inscribed with the sentiment: "Mad about the man."

Her mother believed Audrey was truly mad to have fallen for Ferrer. In her view, he was nothing more than a peculiar-looking, balding, difficult, egomaniacal actor with three failed marriages under his belt and a sinking career on his hands. But doctors had banished the Baroness from Switzerland while Audrey was recuperating, so she knew nothing of their re-ignited courtship.

She also had no idea that Ferrer would fly to Audrey's side the moment he received her present. But he did. And in the middle of the peaceful garden behind Villa Bethiana, Ferrer proposed to Audrey.

She accepted immediately. "But I didn't tell my mother," Audrey recalled. "I knew it was my life and all that, but I still couldn't risk hurting her."

The couple planned a quiet, almost secret wedding, in part to protect the Baroness from the news that would so upset her. But she found out anyway, and reluctantly flew from London to Switzerland to witness the marriage.

Audrey helped to decorate the thirteenth-century chapel near Burgenstock with white carnations and lilies of the valley, her favorite flower. She planned to wear a very simple, very schoolgirlish Pierre Balmain organdy dress with a crown of white roses in her short hair. "I wanted to emphasize purity and devotion," she recalled.

Ferrer, now on location in Sardinia for *Le Madre*, flew in just in time for the ceremony. Ferrer's sister Julia flew in to be a bridesmaid, and English diplomat Sir Neville Bland, former ambassador to the Netherlands, gave the bride away.

Among the other guests were two of Ferrer's children, Pepa and Mark, as well as Paramount's London chief, Richard Mealand.

"I must say it was the happiest day of my life," Audrey recalled. "I guess the hopes and dreams that are pinned on a first marriage are enormous, but so is the glorious anticipation. Marriage with Mel, and the possibility of our having a family, was the most important thing in my life. If we didn't need my income, I would have quit the movies the day we got married."

The happy couple and a few of their friends

and family, including Rev. Maurice Eindiguer, the mesmerizing Protestant minister who married them and spoke about the sanctity of holy matrimony, retreated to a nearby club for a small party of champagne and cake.

The press had by this time gotten word of the ceremony, and several reporters and photographers, at least two of them from the Reuters international wire service, descended upon Burgenstock just as the bride and groom were said to be leaving for a short honeymoon in an undisclosed Italian town.

In fact, they stayed right where they were, holing up nearby in a magnificent chalet owned by hotelier Fritz Frey. While they wrote postcards to friends unable to attend, those same friends, upon hearing of the nuptials, shook their heads in disbelief that two such incompatible people would actually get hitched. "We were different," Audrey recalled. "Even I could admit that then. But we were in love. That was what counted. That was what could make everything else right."

But celebrity intruded on the early stages of their marriage, and it only came knocking on one of their doors. A quiet train ride from Switzerland to Italy did not prepare them for the hordes of photographers and fans who bombarded Audrey at the Rome station. As much as Ferrer wanted to protect his bride, he also needed to protect his own shattered ego from the lack of attention he was receiving.

Besides cementing his relationship with Audrey, the marriage had turned him in the eyes of the public into "Mr. Hepburn." The public expected him to be adoring of his wife, if not fawning. And Ferrer could not be. His own self-esteem was too precarious.

He brought her to a beautiful, isolated farmhouse on the way to Anzio beach, high above the water in the Alban Hills.

"We were always fine when we were alone," Audrey recalled. "And those first few weeks were heaven. I remember we would talk for hours and then say nothing for the same amount of time. Time, in fact, was irrelevant. It felt all speeded up, and then it felt like everything was now. There was no yesterday and no tomorrow. It was only the present, and the present was perfect."

Outside their idyllic compound, armed guards patrolled the grounds to prevent the locustlike swarm of paparazzi from zooming in on intimate moments. Thick grapevines and flowering bougainvillea helped to shelter the couple from inquiring eyes, but some reporters were able to sneak peaks and chronicle the loving way their fingers touched and the gentle caresses of Mel's palm on Audrey's head. Because of Audrey's fame, the interest in the couple was equivalent to the attention later paid to Grace Kelly and Prince Rainier of Monaco.

"I forgot to say that we weren't alone at all," Audrey said with a smile. "We had a donkey, several doves, a bunch of cats, and a couple of dogs. I was in heaven."

But the idyll was soon to be broken. Discussions were under way to find a film project to star both husband and wife. After three weeks of bliss, the couple returned to Italy, where Mel finished *Le Madre*.

The trouble was, nobody really wanted the husband. But Audrey and Ferrer became a package deal upon marriage. And if you wanted the wide-eyed pixie for one of your films, you had to take the dour-faced Svengali, too.

Perhaps because fame had made her even more nervous than usual, perhaps because Ferrer was assuming more control than was appropriate, Audrey began to exhibit visible signs of neurosis. She refused to leave the house and had trouble eating. "The only project that interested me at all was the film version of *Ondine*," she recalled. "I was hot on that because I loved doing the play and of course I could do this with Mel again. Besides, it had all this great romantic wish fulfillment for me: If I could do the movie with Mel, maybe we could re-create the wonderful times together we had doing the play."

Instead, Paramount offered Audrey a movie on her own, *House of Mist*. She turned it down. She was hoping now that she and her husband could mount *Ondine* in London to help drum up interest in it as a movie vehicle. She became single-minded in the desire to resurrect the play, and now began to believe Elstree would accept it as part of her movie commitment to the studio.

"I just knew that if the public could see Mel at his best, as I saw him, they would love him as much as me. Why, they would love him more! That's what I wanted. I was uncomfortable getting the lion's share of attention, and I knew if we could do a film of *Ondine*, he would be better appreciated. It was for my benefit, too, if he were better appreciated: I wouldn't have to pay so much attention to him myself!"

But by all accounts, Audrey luxuriated in indulging Ferrer's every whim. It seemed as if her happiness was dependent on his. In October 1954, she was in for a brutal surprise when she traveled without him to the Netherlands while he was finishing up *Le Madre*.

"It was to be a charity event for Dutch war invalids. How could I refuse?" she recalled.

"But I never dreamed so many people could make so much noise. I was petrified. In a department store in Amsterdam, I was almost trampled to death by thousands of screaming teenage girls.

"I kept thinking that if Mel were with me, he could control the chaos. Isn't that odd? Of course, he couldn't have done much to quiet that mob, but I invested so much power in him as my husband. I felt he could do anything. And I guess I was disappointed when he didn't swoop down like Superman and save me from the mob."

Ever since her father's early abandonment, Audrey had looked for a replacement, a man who could take care of her every need. Ferrer's domineering ways initially made him appear to be a likely father substitute for Audrey.

Of course, that was not ultimately possible. But for a short time — an idyllic few months — Audrey felt that it was. In October 1954, Audrey became pregnant and all was right with the world.

"There is nothing more important to me than having given birth," she has often said when asked about her most important accomplishment. "The thing is, I have always felt that way. With every woman it is different, I know this. I don't judge.

"Or at least I try not to. But I truly cannot imagine anything — anything at all — being more important in a woman's life than the baby she raises. I'm sure I'm very narrow-minded here; I know there are millions of women — childless and not — who have other priorities. But for me, it was never a choice. I wanted to have babies more than anything else, and I had so much difficulty having them."

Their Christmas season that year was one of the most tranquil holidays Audrey ever spent. It was reported in the newspapers that they gave each other matching blue and yellow cashmere sweaters. "That was true," Audrey said. "What we didn't reveal is that we had the tiniest little baby sweater knitted to match ours. It finally felt like the two of us were becoming a family."

Chapter 15

In the summer of 1954, when Carlo Ponti and Dino de Laurentiis asked Audrey to star in their $6 million epic film version of Tolstoy's *War and Peace*, she requested that Ferrer be given a part.

Her desire to help her husband was not unusual, but the anxiety which accompanied it certainly was. She made it clear she wouldn't even consider taking the role of Natasha unless Ferrer costarred with her. Just a year into her marriage, Audrey was becoming distraught over trying to boost her husband's sagging ego and preserve their tenuous connection.

She hemmed and hawed at length before agreeing to do the film. In October, when she realized she was pregnant, she seriously thought about canceling her commitment, but her ironclad rule about professionalism in the face of duty in a field rife with broken promises helped her to stick to her agreement.

"I wanted Audrey right from the start," said Dino de Laurentiis. "I felt her girlish charm and wide-eyed naïveté would do much to enhance the character of Natasha. I also thought that Mel would be wonderful. He had a brooding quality that gave everything he did that added dimension of soulfulness. I thought it would be perfect. But when Audrey announced she was pregnant, I had this sinking feeling in my gut. By the time we were scheduled to begin filming, she would begin showing. I was sure of that, no matter how skinny she was. And my concept of Natasha was completely childlike; I couldn't have any womanly curves. I felt in an awful position. I didn't know what to do.

"Audrey would come over sometimes, and my kids would just flock to her, and she to them. It was astounding, honestly, how she communicated with even the littlest among them. All this time, I knew she was finally letting go a little, finally ready to be a little more spontaneous. And it was all because of the prospect of having a child. She was practicing with my children, and she was doing a wonderful job. But I still didn't know what I was going to do about *War and Peace*. I needed an overload of virginity — the quintessential innocent — for the girl who was to wander among Napoleon's troops, and all of that had to show in her physical innocence."

In March of 1955, Audrey experienced premature labor pains and suffered a painful miscarriage. "I wanted to cancel the movie," she said. "I wanted to cancel my life. But I moved forward for Mel. He thought that *War and Peace* would help me get over my grief and I felt it would help him recapture his career. I'm not sure it accomplished either of those goals, but it helped pass a desolate time and brought us closer together."

The kinks in the new wide-screen technique, VistaVision, were not ironed out by the time director King Vidor began filming *War and Peace*, and the magnitude of the venture — six screenwriters, four thousand guns, six thousand rifles, seven thousand costumes (requiring more than one hundred thousand buttons) and enough artificial snow for two blizzards — added to the difficulties. Consequently, intimate scenes of personal interchange were often lost in the maze of props, settings, and visual effects.

Although the battle scenes between the French and Russian armies are stirring and faultlessly executed, the small moments shared between major characters are lost in the wide-frame technique.

"I had such high hopes for *War and Peace* after we finished filming," Audrey recalled. "But in an epic, the characters are less important than the historical sweep. In many frames, it seems we humans are lost in the vistas. And there was just so much going on, you almost need a map to follow it all."

Vidor had a hard time eliciting strong emotion from Audrey in *War and Peace*. She seemed to have no problem at all with the scenes in which she depicted a somewhat bratty, self-indulgent young woman, but when she was called upon to portray desolation, it was extremely difficult for her.

"I was uncomfortable with so much going on within one film," she said, by way of explanation. "I was still in profound mourning for the loss of my child, and I wasn't able to exhibit too much emotion. I was afraid it wouldn't stop coming. I wanted to feel in control of my life. Maybe Vidor knew this, because he downplayed the emotions anyway. He kept telling us the whole point of this movie was to prove that movies were still contenders, that television couldn't compete on every level. Television clearly couldn't compete in the area of visual effects back then, and *War and Peace* was made as a kind of showcase for big effects. I got the impression the characters were secondary to the big battle scenes.

"We couldn't compete with those anyway. I mean next to a mammoth battle, a few tears, however heartfelt, are going to look piddling anyway.

"For me, of course, the movie grew boring when Mel's character died," Audrey recalled. "But that speaks more about my desire to see him fully utilized on-screen than anything about the success of the movie. This was a film I decided to do because we could act in it together. It helped pass the time when time was interminable."

"Too much war," wrote one critic, "not enough peace."

The same could be said for Audrey's marriage.

Audrey found that her desire to share her success with Mel could not overcome the very real problems in their marriage. Matters were not helped by the fact that the multimillion-dollar blockbuster *War and Peace* was an incontrovertible dud with critics and the public alike.

Chapter 16

As so often happens, Audrey was feeling extremely low while her fans were putting her higher and higher on the stardom pedestal. In a poll conducted in fifty countries, the Foreign Film Association had voted her the most popular actress in the world. Movies offers poured in. She had to hire two part-time secretaries just to open the fan mail. But underneath the glittering exterior, Audrey was in pain. She was still distraught over the loss of her baby, which she finally admitted accounted for her distracted performance in *War and Peace*.

"I really never thought I'd be able to act again," she recalled. "Mel and I were experiencing a lot of tension at home, until I realized I really had no desire to do anything. People always get the impression that he ruled my life. But to some extent, and especially during my 'down' days, I asked him to. I couldn't make decisions at all after the miscarriage. I wanted to be told what to do. He told me. He was my husband,

and I trusted him.

"Tennessee Williams and [producer] Hal Wallis flew to Rome, where we were renting the Alban Hills villa, to try to persuade me to do *Summer and Smoke*. It was too sad a role for me at the time, this spinsterish school-teacher who finally discovers love and doesn't realize it. But I didn't know how to let them know. I had been leading them on. So when they arrived, I desperately wanted Mel to turn them down for me. It was just my luck that he was very late that night, and I was stuck talking a blue streak — talking about anything and everything but the subject — until he got home. He was pretty abrupt with them. He suggested I choose something light for my next role. The truth is, it [his suggestion] sure sounded good to me."

Audrey made up her mind about *Funny Face* in two short hours. "I felt I didn't sing well enough, or dance well enough, but the idea of working with Fred Astaire clinched it for me." Her first movie musical, it would become a cult classic with the fashion industry and insure her popularity for years to come.

Paramount had bought a property called *Wedding Day*, developed by Leonard Gershe about his friend, photographer Richard Avedon. The studio retitled it *Funny Face*, the name of a 1920s stage musical starring

Fred Astaire and his sister Adele.

In the 1957 movie version of *Funny Face*, Astaire plays fashion photographer Dick Avery, and for verisimilitude, Avedon was hired as a "visual consultant." He insured that the movie was not "painfully silly," he said, "and it was not. I made sure most of the things that happened could at least have really happened. But I found the whole piece so charming, so light and refreshing, that I didn't have too many objections. How could you, when you got to see Audrey Hepburn every day?"

Astaire, too, would only consider Audrey for the part. But there were many complications, including the sale of the option on the property to different movie companies over the years. Eventually, the entire production wound up where it began, at Paramount. Stanley Donen, veteran director of musicals, was chosen to oversee the effort.

"I was worried about filming in Paris," Audrey recalled. "I wanted so much to do the movie, but I didn't want to leave Mel for an extended period. Eventually, he got *Elena et Les Hommes* with Jean Renoir, so everything worked itself out," she said. "Everything was always working itself out, but sometimes the effort was enormous."

In Hollywood, where she traveled to bone up on dance classes and shoot the interior scenes, Audrey and Ferrer rented a small house in Malibu owned by director Anatole Litvak and furnished it with candlesticks, cachepots, silver framed photos, and blue glass vases from Switzerland. "I always took as many of my possessions with me when we had to rent places," she recalled. "It made me feel secure. This time around, I really needed that feeling. I was only twenty-seven, but I was a little creaky. I mean, I hadn't been at the barre for years, and my out-of-practice showed."

Audrey worked with dance director Eugene Loring on technique and stamina, but the real creative influence was Astaire himself.

Thirty years later, at the celebration of Astaire's Lifetime Achievement Award for his contribution to movie musicals, Audrey recalled their first meeting. It was at one of the early rehearsals of *Funny Face*.

"I remember he was wearing a yellow shirt, gray flannel, a red scarf knotted around his waist instead of a belt, and the famous feet were clad in soft moccasins and pink socks. He was also wearing that irresistible smile.

"One look at this most debonair, elegant, and distinguished of legends and I could feel myself turn to solid lead. My heart sank into my two left feet.

"Then suddenly I felt a hand around my

waist and, with his inimitable grace and lightness, Fred literally swept me off my feet. [Astaire has been quoted as saying that Audrey was shaking so much, he didn't have a choice.] I experienced the thrill that all women at some point in their lives have dreamed of — to dance just once with Fred Astaire."

Astaire, a notorious perfectionist, was gentle with Audrey because he knew that enthusiasm would win more hard work from her than criticism. He also was well aware of her burgeoning popularity and didn't want to risk losing her due to her insecurities. Lastly, he sensed his own days as a leading song-and-dance man coming to an end. He was fifty-seven when filming began (Audrey was thirty years his junior) and he wanted the final years of his career to be as stress-free as possible.

The *Funny Face* plot is simple, if a little simpleminded. A satire that pokes fun at the world of intellectual pursuits as well as the emptiness of the fashion industry, its story line incorporates both.

Magazine editor Maggie Prescott (Kay Thompson), based on *Vogue*'s Diana Vreeland, comes up with the idea to do a fashion spread that shows women can be beautiful as well as brainy.

She and photographer Dick Avery (Astaire), along with a bunch of the usual witless blond models, decide to shoot their story at a Greenwich Village bookshop. Jo Stockton (Audrey), the clerk at the store, becomes incensed when they disrupt her quiet and mess up her rows of books.

One of the early difficulties was making Audrey look unattractive for the early scenes. "I didn't think that was going to be hard at all, and it really wasn't," Audrey recalled. "But I did have to look vastly different before I became a model. [Designer] Edith [Head] and [couturier] Hubert [de Givenchy] focused on colors. In the early parts of the movie, I am dressed in drab, muddy tones."

In one scene, recalled director Stanley Donen, "Audrey and I agreed that she would wear black, tight-fitting pants, a black sweater, and black shoes. That was one of her normal outfits, so I didn't think it would be too much to ask. Then I casually mentioned that I wanted her to wear white socks with it, and she was stunned. 'Absolutely not!' she said. 'It will cut the line at my feet!' I said, 'If you don't wear the white socks, you'll fade into the background, there will be no definition to your movement, and the dance sequence will be bland and dull.'

"She burst into tears and ran into her dressing room. After a little while, she regained her composure, put on the white socks, returned to the set, and went ahead without a whimper. She was a professional through and through. Later, when she saw the sequence, she sent me a note saying, 'You were right about the socks. Love, Audrey.'

In the movie, while Dick is helping her clean up the mess his models have made, she tells him about "empathacalism," the French philosophy she is studying. He, of course, has little interest in this obscure cult, but he does like Jo. He suggests to Maggie that she use her for a spread to be shot in France. She agrees. He suggests to Jo that she take the assignment so that she can meet her fellow students and teachers on their home turf, especially Professor Flostre (Michel Auclair).

Everything is extremely neat and tidy, just as plots should be in movie musicals, but what distinguishes *Funny Face* from many of its brethren are the delightfully real and visually striking sequences.

Right after Dick leaves the bookstore and Jo is alone, she walks among the dusty, dark shelves, herself dressed in dark neutrals, when she comes upon a long, colorful scarf left behind by the visitors. Thinking of the kiss Dick has just stolen from her, she drapes the scarf around herself and begins to sing "How Long Has This Been Going On?" Dressed in muddy blacks and browns and grays, her small, sinewy physique is the perfect frame for the colorful scarf and makes the scarf look as if it is dancing on its own. It is a perfect moment in film, as is the opening musical number in which Maggie sings "Think Pink!"

The other early scenes, in which Jo, Maggie, and Dick first iron out the details for the European trip, offer a case study in conveying different personalities merely through body language. The studious Jo (head bent) contrasts easily with the exuberant Maggie (hands flying), who is very different from the romantic Dick (soulful gazes).

There is not much idle chat in *Funny Face*, leaving more time for the marvelous songs and dances and the wonderfully choreographed nonmusical sequences, which play like dances without formal steps.

When Dick and Jo arrive in the City of Light and sing "Bonjour, Paris," we begin to fall in love with Audrey just as we are finally warming up to Jo, her bookish character. It's a wonderful synchronicity, intensifying audience identification with the skinny bookworm who turns into a stunning model.

Dick photographs her all over Paris in the wonderful Duval creations (made for the screen by the inimitable Givenchy) and she gradually begins to fall in love with him, returning his feelings. In her scenes as a model, she has never looked more lovely — except to Givenchy, who remembers that when she briefly worked as a runway model for him in 1951, he had never seen a more beautiful woman. But to most of us who witness Audrey in his magnificent dresses in *Funny Face*, she could never look more sweetly elegant.

It is easy to accept her effect upon Dick in the movie. And while he is snapping Jo, dressed as a bride, outside a small church in Chantilly, she tells him she loves him. He sings "He Loves and She Loves," and the movie soars into romantic heaven.

In fact, the scene was nearly impossible to film, thanks to the torrents of rain that turned the ground to mud. "We had to dance down a lawn and through a garden," Audrey recalled. "Every time we began, one of us would sink lower in the ground. I nearly fell three times. Fred and I took to saying, 'Here's mud in your eye' under our breath, and then we'd get the giggles. It was quite a long day!"

Along with other George and Ira Gershwin songs that are performed flawlessly, "How Long Has This Been Going On?" and " 'S Wonderful" helped establish a charming screen chemistry between the two stars, despite their considerable age difference.

The plot encourages Professor Flostre to act as an obstacle to their budding romance. But when Jo realizes that he is flirting with her, she becomes incensed. "I came here to talk to you as a philosopher, and you are talking like a man," she says, before hitting him over the head with a statue.

Of course, Dick doesn't realize that Jo has spurned her teacher's advances, and he forlornly decides to fly back to the States without her. But in a last-minute revelation, he learns the truth and searches for Jo all over Paris.

He finds her in the church where they danced to "He Loves and She Loves." In a reprise, they sing " 'S Wonderful," and gently float away on a raft.

"I am fairly proud of my voice in *Funny Face*," Audrey said. "A lot of people don't realize the movie wasn't dubbed. But Kay [costar Thompson] persuaded me I could hold my own. I'm so glad she did. I was so afraid of performing with Astaire that I felt I couldn't do anything. But I always went through enormous insecurities before I actually got to work on a picture. Once I got started, they would always melt away."

Pounds also melted away during the grueling summer shoot. Audrey had again stopped eating. By the end of production, she had lost seventeen pounds and weighed only ninety-two. The Baroness flew in from London and brought with her bars of chocolate like the kind that were given to Audrey by the United Nations rescue team after World War II.

She refused to eat them.

Chapter 17

Almost as soon as she finished *Funny Face*, Audrey began *Love in the Afternoon*.

Exhausted, malnourished, and worried about how independent-minded director Billy Wilder was going to take to her husband's constant "advice," Audrey couldn't help but recall that the last time she'd worked with Wilder, on *Sabrina*, she had fallen in love with Bill Holden.

Meanwhile, Wilder was a little concerned about Audrey's weight. "She's a wispy little thing," he said, "but you're really in the presence of somebody when you see that girl."

It's a pity Audrey didn't feel the confidence in herself that she generated in others. "I kept having this premonition that Gary Cooper, whom I had always admired, was going to turn out to hate me like Humphrey Bogart," she said. "I was working myself into a frenzy. Mel wasn't much help because frankly, he was incensed that I was even thinking of the time when I met Bill Holden. Mel was a jealous husband, and I always loved that about him."

The story of *Love in the Afternoon* was the most explicitly sexual Audrey had ever done. As the Parisian schoolgirl Ariane Chavasse, Audrey had to bring to the part a knowing flirtatiousness that would help seduce the aging American roué Frank Flannagan (Gary Cooper) without making her appear like an out-and-out Lolita.

"I was more worried about how I looked when I started this movie than any other film of my career," Audrey recalled. "I don't know — maybe it was because I lost so much weight during *Funny Face*, but I felt particularly ugly when we began filming.

"Everybody kept telling me not to worry, since my costar was so much older, but I thought Coop's crags gave him character, while I just looked washed-out and hollow-eyed."

Wilder recalled the first week of filming. "You looked around and suddenly there was this dazzling creature looking like a wild-eyed doe prancing in the forest. Everybody on the set was in love with her within five minutes."

Still, she did not love herself. Herb Sterne, the publicist on the movie, remembered that she drove him crazy with demands. "She wanted approval on all the stills that we sent out, which was not unusual, but she nearly refused to sit for any stills!

"I remember we had to almost hold her down to take some shots, and I had to bring a whole rack of clothes out for her to decide. Then we'd paint the backdrops for the photos as she was getting changed. It was just awful. She was in a dreadful state, fretting and fussing all the time. At one point, she became obsessed with her nostrils and was convinced they flared too wide in some of the early scenes. She begged us to reshoot, but of course we didn't. I must admit, we did try to humor her, though. We led her to believe we would reshoot at the end. She was so upset, there was very little else we could do."

Aware that his wife was indulging in one of her bouts of neurosis, Ferrer ingeniously gave her a gift to take her mind off herself. When she walked into their suite at the Hotel Raphael one day, a tiny dog yelped from a bed Ferrer had made from Audrey's old stockings and underwear.

Mr. Famous, known to his intimates as "Famous," had the desired effect on Audrey. The little Yorkshire terrier terrorized the staff at the hotel with his insistent bark, but he would spend hours licking the soles of Audrey's feet while she petted his head. It was, by all accounts, a mutual admiration society unmatched in history.

"I lavished attention on that puppy," Audrey recalled. "I am a frugal person, but I bought Famous the most expensive collars, the best cuts of meat, the most gentle shampoos. I was out of my mind with love for that little dog. I guess it took my mind off my fears about meeting the great Gary Cooper."

She really had nothing to worry about. Wilder, aware that Audrey was intimidated about meeting the legendary star of *High Noon*, scheduled their first meeting to coincide with the filming of a fox-trot sequence.

Coop couldn't dance. "His stumbling around was the best thing that could have happened in the beginning of the movie," Audrey recalled. "I had to help him. Wilder suggested he take dancing lessons. The whole episode just put me at ease."

Although he dressed beautifully in Savile Row-tailored suits and paisley ascots, Cooper looked much older than his fifty-six years and scared Wilder into worrying that censors would balk at his screen romance with Audrey.

Based on Claude Anet's sophisticated, witty novel *Ariane, Love in the Afternoon* was revised by Wilder and coscreenwriter I.A.L. Diamond to include a chaperon character of sorts. They wrote in the character of Ariane's father Claude Chavasse (Maurice Chevalier), who plays a private investigator delving into the life of the millionaire playboy with whom his daughter is infatuated.

Given that Audrey had just come off *Funny Face*, another movie about a May/December romance, and knowing that she had played a similar role of a somewhat calculating ingenue in Wilder's *Sabrina*, it's interesting to note that Wilder had some real trepidation this time around.

"It all came down to Coop's astounding good looks," Audrey recalled. "He was just so great-looking, I think Wilder thought the audience might hold it against him; they wouldn't believe my character engineered the whole romance. For once, I understood why good looks could be a liability."

Relying on his background as a coscreenwriter for the great director of comedy Ernst Lubitsch, Wilder paid tribute to his mentor here, going so far as to cast Cooper, the star of Lubitsch's 1938 film *Bluebeard's Eighth Wife*.

Wilder's revision of the basic story of *Ariane* is ingenious. We meet Ariane (Audrey) first. In the opening scenes, the wildly fantasizing daughter of private eye Claude Chavasse (Maurice Chevalier) is surreptitiously paging through her father's marital files and becomes enamored of Frank Flannagan (Gary Cooper).

Flannagan is a man-and-a-half about town,

indulging in numerous relationships with married women, the better for him to avoid commitment.

As Ariane reads on, she discovers that one of her father's clients plans to catch Flannagan in the act with his wife and shoot him on the spot.

She decides to intervene, rushing to Flannagan's hotel bedroom and replacing his lady friend just as her jealous — and perplexed — husband appears.

He is captivated by his mysterious young savior, and the two begin to meet during the afternoons over the next couple of months. Their relationship develops slowly and believably, until it's clear it has come to a full boil.

The trouble is, Flannagan doesn't know anything about his secretive lover, including her last name. He hires private eye Claude Chavasse to uncover her identity.

Wilder had wanted to make the movie for years, primarily because it explored a theme he enjoyed: the way a free-spirited woman can draw a self-absorbed man out of his shell. But casting had always presented a problem for him.

With his three leads, he achieved a perfect mesh of romantic love tempered by fatherly concern. Cinematographer William Mellor's muted lighting and use of haunting silhouettes contrasted with the frothy comedic elements of *Love in the Afternoon* and gave the movie heft, while set designer Alexander Trauner worked with real Parisian sites, including the Ritz Hotel, even somehow enhancing their historic beauty.

It is a stunning achievement, and a movie that is inexplicably underappreciated.

"Once we got going, we all had a wonderful time making the movie," Audrey recalled. "We'd all go out for drinks after a hard day of filming, and unlike *Sabrina*, everybody on this set got along famously. We'd go to a place that made the best martinis in the world — dry and cold as can be without freezing. Wilder would tease me mercilessly.

"In the movie, there's this running gag about Flannagan's private gypsy band that follows him on all his escapades playing 'Fascination' every time he meets a new woman. Well, Wilder told me he chose that song because it was playing the first time he ever made love. That made me so embarrassed, even though I later found out he made up the whole thing, that I couldn't look at him if he was giving me some advice when that song was playing. And it seemed 'Fascination' never stopped playing. I think Wilder wanted me to gain some self-confidence, learn to rely more on my own instincts than his."

During the making of the movie, Audrey did begin to branch out a little, to test her wings. She openly enjoyed the caresses from Cooper, telling Wilder that she felt guilty for accepting a paycheck for so sweet an assignment. Cooper echoed her delight. "I've been in pictures for thirty years," he said, "and I've never had a more enthusiastic leading lady than Audrey. She puts more life and energy into her acting than anyone I've ever met."

Although they enjoyed and respected one another, there was never a hint of romantic involvement, despite the fact that Audrey was alone at night for the first time since she had married.

Ferrer was away during the week, filming *The Vintage* in the south of France, and Audrey finally began to see she could live very nicely, and less stressfully, when they did not spend twenty-four hours a day together.

He had often engineered her interviews with the press and controlled them to such a degree that Audrey came across as an aloof, almost stupid, woman, but now she was observed by several reporters cursing and kicking up her heels at a little drinking party organized by Wilder.

When Ferrer got wind of her behavior, he chastised her royally. "You are ruining all I have created," he said. "I think it's time you take a little rest."

Chapter 18

"You must learn to bend a little, or you will break," says one of the older nuns to the character Audrey would next portray, the headstrong Sister Luke in *The Nun's Story*.

It was a lesson Audrey would try to learn, without lasting results, for her entire life.

For although she felt stronger and more confident than ever while she worked on *Love in the Afternoon* and saw her husband only on weekends for some relaxing times in Saint-Tropez, Audrey also felt guilty about the physical distance between them.

"I know it was foolish, but it's just the way I'm built," she recalled. "We were getting along beautifully when we saw one another less frequently, there were none of the daily tensions and annoyances, but I still felt something was wrong with us if we couldn't be at each other's side all the time. And I think Mel agreed with me. I think that's why he worked so hard to get *Mayerling* [in which they costarred] off the ground."

So almost as soon as she had tentatively

begun to cut the cord to her husband, Audrey rewrapped it even tighter, afraid that their marriage was an all-or-nothing-at-all proposition.

In the beginning of 1957, at the height of her popularity, Audrey announced that she was taking a year off. She turned down incredible movie offers: *The Diary of Anne Frank*, what would eventually become *The Sound of Music*, and *A Certain Smile*, a film based on Françoise Sagan's bittersweet novella. The stage beckoned as well. She was asked to replace Diane Cilento in the London West End musical *Zuleika*, based on a novel by Max Beerbohm, before it transferred to Broadway, but she turned down that offer as well. Instead, in Burgenstock, she planted roses, cooked Ferrer simple meals, and rested a lot while news of her continuing popularity slowly filtered into Switzerland.

Society photographer Antony Beauchamp included her in a photo essay called "The Ten Loveliest Women." The New York Dress Institute voted her the sixth-best-dressed woman in the world. *Daily News* columnist Cholly Knickerbocker named her one of the ten most fascinating women in the world.

"I read about those honors as if they were being bestowed on another woman," she recalled. "Always when I stopped working, I

214

felt very far away from the Audrey Hepburn of the marquee. I had an awfully hard time incorporating myself into my work, and vice versa, so when I read somewhere that somebody thought I was a marvelous dresser, I realized I thought the clothes were nice, too, but I didn't take any credit for them. In any case, beautiful dresses always seemed like costumes to me. I knew I could carry them off, but they weren't my attire of choice. That would be old, loose jeans, too short, pants that I could garden in."

Around the time Audrey exiled herself in Switzerland in temporary retirement, she discovered that her father was still alive. "My mother had told me in passing that he had died, but for some reason Mel didn't believe this, and he did his own snooping. He discovered my father was alive, in Ireland, near Dublin. I was the happiest I had been in a while on the day I flew to meet him. But then reality set in. He was aloof when we met. I felt bad about interfering with his new life. The meeting I had hoped for my whole life turned into one of my biggest disappointments. We didn't have a lot to say to one another. I never heard from him again."

To take her mind off her personal troubles, Audrey decided to travel with her husband when he was offered a supporting role in the film version of Hemingway's novel *The Sun Also Rises*.

"I went with him on location," Audrey recalled, "and I had the time of my life. It was the first time in our marriage that I felt like a real wife. I was finally in the supporting role, and I adored it. I would go shopping in Mexico with Ava Gardner for little trinkets while Mel was doing a little scene, and at night, Errol Flynn and Ava and Tyrone Power and I would all go out for a meal. It felt normal. It was new for me. My husband was at work during the day and I stayed home. It was a division of labor that made sense."

It was probably as attractive a situation as it was because it followed one of the truly disastrous events of their careers.

On New Year's Day 1957, after having asked Audrey not to take on any new projects for a year, Ferrer flew her to New York to begin production with him on *Mayerling*, a ninety-minute NBC special about the site in Austria where, in 1889, Crown Prince Rudolf of the Hapsburg Empire was found dead in a double-suicide pact with his mistress, Mary Vetsera.

Given their own marital tensions, portraying the doomed couple was an ironic choice of roles for Audrey and Ferrer, but as usual, Audrey acquiesced to her husband's wishes.

Director Anatole Litvak, who got to know the couple when they rented his Malibu home while Audrey was making *Funny Face*, had always harbored a secret wish to do *Mayerling* with her. He had directed the original movie in 1936 in France that had made stars of Charles Boyer and Danielle Darrieux, and he only thought about doing it again the first time he met Audrey.

"It was not like me to repeat myself," he told an interviewer in 1957, "but when I met Audrey Hepburn, I knew I had no choice. She was aristocratic and vulnerable, full of laughter and full of sorrow, just as I pictured the prince's mistress."

Ferrer, in the role of the Crown Prince, would not have been Litvak's first pick, but he didn't have a choice. Audrey stipulated that she would play the part only if her husband was given an equal role — with equal billing. Although Ferrer presumably wanted Audrey to take a rest, his own career superseded those desires. He had been dealing for several years with Audrey's neuroses and insecurities and he desperately needed some validation. Sadly, he was no longer considered leading-man material, and he had to fight long and hard for roles, using whatever means available to him, including his popular wife. And he truly believed that if he worked closely enough with

Audrey, he could monitor her moods.

Her depression over the loss of her baby continued, and Ferrer began to worry at the extent to which Audrey lavished attention on the Yorkshire terrier. So did director Litvak.

"I had an inordinate amount of trouble getting Mel and Audrey to create 'heat' on-screen," Litvak recalled. "Audrey seemed to have a better rapport with that dog of hers."

In fact, in a photo in *Life* magazine taken on the set of *Mayerling*, Litvak is hugging Audrey as Ferrer looks on perplexed. The caption reads: "Litvak as lover shows Ferrer how he should hold his wife, Audrey, to get the best effect at romantic scenes."

The difficulties in shooting appeared in the finished product. When NBC aired *Mayerling* as part of its *Producer's Showcase* series, critics panned it mercilessly. "The lovers seemed more fated to bore each other to death than to end their illicit alliance in a murder-suicide pact," wrote Sheilah Graham. "I knew the final outcome from my history books," noted Joe Hyams, "and I was counting the minutes to the inevitable."

Audrey was upset by the criticism, but she felt relieved that, because of it, she didn't have to go straight back to work. Other projects that were being considered for Audrey and Ferrer were immediately nixed by Paramount.

The joint efforts that had been under consideration before the airing of *Mayerling* included productions of *Look Homeward, Angel*, based on Thomas Wolfe's stunning novel, and Jean Anouilh's *The Lark*.

Back in Switzerland, she tended her roses and tried to conceive. When Ferrer recommended she read The Nun's Story, a semibiographical account of the life of Marie Louise Habets written by her friend Kathryn C. Hulme, she jumped at the chance to get out of herself and her problems.

But the story of the Belgian girl, Gabrielle Van Der Mal, who must choose between following her heart and following the rules was close enough to Audrey's own emotional tug-of-war that she felt moved to explore the possibility of bringing it to the screen.

A few phone calls later, she discovered that director Fred Zinnemann, who had overseen Gary Cooper in *High Noon*, had been interested in *The Nun's Story* since the book was first published. He couldn't get the project off the ground, however; every studio had turned him down, feeling the story of a nun had little commercial appeal. But with the addition of Audrey to the project, executives at the movie companies changed their minds.

Zinnemann credited Audrey with interesting Warner Brothers in the project. "It was

Audrey's name alone which made the deal possible," he said.

But Audrey herself was not fully convinced that she wanted to do the role. As usual, she would go through the motions of enthusiasm before the deal was actually signed, but only after she had won over the other principals would she begin any serious consideration of it herself.

"I was attracted to this property more than any other film script I'd ever read," Audrey recalled. "Part of me felt it might be a defilement to even attempt to bring it to the screen, because the words were so heartfelt. But I was really moved by the story, completely swept up in Gabrielle's wrenching decision. I loved that we shared a birthplace, and that one of the more dramatic episodes of the story took place during World War II when the Nazis terrorized Europe.

"But I was also traumatized by the idea of reliving my own horrors if I did this movie. I had suffered off and on from flashbacks of those times when my relatives were killed by the Nazis, and I wanted to do nothing to possibly encourage those nightmarish memories. Again, I was in a quandary. I loved the property, was a little frightened of its power, and realized there was no part for Mel. I would be away from him for a long time, in Africa of all faraway places, and I was in a state where I didn't know if that would be bad for our marriage or good."

Her agent, Kurt Frings, who rarely pressured Audrey to do anything, exerted his influence on her to do *The Nun's Story*. "He told me it would be the role of a lifetime," she said. "How could I argue with that?"

Nervous about leaving Ferrer, nervous about her delicate health in a tropical climate, she waffled about committing completely to the project.

"But Mel was encouraging, too," she recalled. "He was trying to get together *Green Mansions* for the two of us, and he kept insisting that he would keep busy scouting locations in South America for that project while I was in Africa. I really hated the idea of just leaving him in Switzerland with nothing to do. It was a combination of the times — don't forget, it was the fifties — and my own personality, but I had a very difficult time not taking a backseat to my husband. In order for that to happen, he, of course, had to have a project. So as soon as he got confirmation that *Green Mansions* would be a go-ahead, I felt it was my duty to do *The Nun's Story*."

The story itself is a meditation on duty. Gabrielle (Audrey), a devout young Belgian girl who becomes Sister Luke, is torn between helping others as a nurse and heeding her vow of obedience as a nun.

Strong-willed, devoted to both her career and her vocation, Gabrielle is a study in ambivalence, a state of being Audrey knew all too well.

"It was fabulous to get to play a part where the character wasn't sure what she wanted," Audrey recalled. "Most of my roles were depictions of women who knew exactly what they wanted and went out and got it. Well, that wasn't me. I was always more like Sister Luke, always a little unsure."

Director Zinnemann and screenwriter Robert Anderson, who had written *Tea and Sympathy*, insisted on gradually adding dimensions to Gabrielle's personality, letting it grow naturally as she becomes more adult.

In the first half of the movie, Gabrielle and the other "brides of Christ" learn, sometimes painfully, how to follow the rules of their order. They are told to regard the bells that ring to call them to prayer as "the voice of God." They are told when to talk and when not to, when to eat and when to bow their heads and what time to rise and how often to wash. In essence, they are taught to subsume their own personalities to the greater good of God.

Gabrielle's teacher, Mother Emmanuel

(Dame Edith Evans), reminds her that the life she has chosen is not easy, but that humility will aid her in achieving serenity. One senses that the young postulant respects her Mother Superior, but would rather receive a posting to the Belgian Congo than something as ephemeral to her as serenity. Still, she is her own harshest critic, berating herself for questioning the wisdom of her superiors.

With patience, she takes her final vows as Sister Luke and prays until she is finally assigned to Africa, where she is delighted to work from morning until night at a little hospital in the Belgian Congo.

Her superior there, Dr. Fortunati (Peter Finch), is an irreverent, cynical surgeon who laughs to himself over her devotion to the rules of Catholicism. But he witnesses in her the tension between the two parts of herself, and respects her desire to fulfill her obligations as a nun and a nurse.

Among her many fears in tackling the movie, Audrey was petrified of working with the Australian-born Finch. He had been the director's third choice, after Gerard Philipe and Yves Montand of France turned him down.

"I remember hearing all about his womanizing," Audrey said about Finch. "And I had this premonition that he would get a great big kick out of teasing all of us in nuns' habits. It was not what I had in mind for making a movie — sweating in the African heat by day, and sweating under a man's constant flirtation at night. But as it turns out, he was a complete gentleman and a consummate performer. I came to love Finchy on this movie, and I think he came to respect me. We were completely opposite, you see, and a lot of times differences really do complement one another."

Among the other stellar cast members, Dame Peggy Ashcroft as Mother Mathilda and Dame Edith Evans as Mother Emmanuel became close to Audrey during the filming. Rosalie Crutchley, who had a supporting role as Sister Eleanor, remembers the older actresses being mesmerized by Audrey's performance. "I think they wanted to fatten her up a bit, too," Crutchley said. "One of them, I don't remember which, blamed it all on her dog. She thought Audrey did far too much running around after that animal."

After protracted negotiations, Audrey had been able to bring Mr. Famous with her to Africa. The strategy had required consultations with Congolese government officials and lawyers and took several months. Warner Brothers initiated the discussions and took them seriously indeed after Audrey informed the studio that she would back out of the movie if her puppy were not allowed to accompany her. She kept his inoculation papers framed in her dressing room.

In January 1958, after a soggy goodbye to Ferrer (she had planned every one of his meals while she would be away), she began the first leg of her journey, flying from Los Angeles to Paris, where she stayed at a convent in Froyennes.

"It was excellent training," she recalled. "A dose of method acting. I remember best the quiet."

On-screen, that peacefulness was also apparent, especially in contrast to the nervousness of Dr. Fortunati. As Finch played him, he is flabbergasted when Sister Luke faints from hunger on the operating room floor after fasting all morning to take Holy Communion, but it's clear he respects her willpower.

Offscreen, most of the cast members marveled at her stamina as well. The Sabena Guest House, where Zinnemann and his actors were staying while in Stanleyville (now called Kisangani), one of the most populated towns in the Belgian Congo, was nothing more than a series of modest bungalows loosely grouped around a main office.

"It was the opposite of palatial," Dame Peggy Ashcroft said. "It was modest. Very,

225

very modest. But Audrey raved about it — how quaint, how perfect for her dog! When we all could have started to wallow in self-pity, Audrey brought us out. She was the best person to have in primitive surroundings: She was an enthusiast!"

Torrential rains in this equatorial region often postponed production. And when it wasn't raining, it was so humid, it felt like it was raining, "only without the drops," Zinnemann said.

In one scene, Audrey got completely drenched during a day of filming and she couldn't determine if it was sweat or rain that had made her so wet. "My memory is that I was just sopping the whole time, sopping and laughing," she said.

But then a spiritual turning point for Audrey occurred.

Crutchley recalled that Audrey had been "fairly obsessed" with children when they all arrived in the Congo. "She'd talk on and on about my children," Crutchley said. "How beautiful they were, how angelic. She'd finger their pictures so carefully, as if she could somehow hurt them. I sensed so strongly that she wanted babies more than anything else in her life."

But when a local photographer thanked Audrey for posing for him by giving her a beautiful doll, she lost control. "I hate dolls," she screamed at him. "Dolls look like dead babies!" Then she began to weep and left the set. When Ferrer heard about her outburst, he considered flying to her side, but Zinnemann told him that he'd be more of a distraction than a help.

But she experienced a profound lifting of her depression after she visited a leper colony at Yalisombo, fifty miles up the Congo River.

"We started out very early in the morning," Audrey recalled, "and from the moment I got up, I knew it was going to be a momentous day. We traveled by ferry, very slowly it seemed, and I could hear every bird and every monkey in the jungle. I was entranced. I felt, as they say, one with nature; I really did.

"Time passed in a very strange way after that. I can't say it did pass. I was in sort of a daze. I remember meeting Dr. Stanley Browne, the missionary who started the leper colony twenty years before, and I saw this halo around his head. I did! I hate for my vision to be so clichéd, but so be it.

"It was Sunday and we all went to church. It was the most moving experience of my life. Everybody spoke different languages, different dialects, but at the end, when they played Beethoven's *Ode to Joy*, I felt as if a great weight was gone. I was grateful for my life, my ability to influence people, my talents, my enormous love. I had faith in God. If He wanted me to have a baby, it would happen. I wasn't going to worry about it from here on in."

Despite her own personal joy, Audrey had to depict enormous internal eruptions when Sister Luke is ordered to leave her beloved Africa. But World War II has broken out, and she's needed at a hospital near the border with Holland.

Audrey gives a breathtaking performance as Sister Luke, easily and seamlessly conveying her passions and her doubts. Because she is on the screen so much, the slightest false note would have sounded glaringly. Yet there are only the sound of the bells that call her to her duty to God.

Like Audrey, she feels another duty as well: to her country. After the Nazis kill her father, Sister Luke becomes more and more devoted to the Belgian underground resistance, while her superiors advise her to remain neutral. Yet she wants to seek revenge for her father's death. She cannot forgive the Germans. She realizes she is unworthy of her vocation.

The final scene echoes the first one in the movie. Sister Luke removes the ring that celebrated her as a nun. It is the same gold band that we saw her lovingly twirl in the opening sequence of the movie, and it is a powerful reminder that some commitments are better off broken.

In a pattern that was painfully evident to everyone but her, Audrey moved from her personal triumph in *The Nun's Story* to the dreadful experience of *Green Mansions* in a valiant yet futile effort to make her husband feel useful.

"Mel was so excited about the movie that his enthusiasm rubbed off on me, too," Audrey recalled. "Of course, I was pretty sick. I had developed a case of kidney stones in the Belgian Congo and I was recuperating in Rome when Mel flew in and asked if he should postpone. No way! He had worked too hard for all of it to be lost over a little pain in my back," she said, downplaying the excruciating suffering she experienced. "We would move forward," she said, "because I said so! It was a nice sense of power."

Ferrer had loved the "Romance of the Tropical Forest," the subtitle of W. H. Hudson's *Green Mansions*, ever since he'd read the book as a Princeton undergraduate. But he was not the first filmmaker who wanted to bring it to the screen. It already had a checkered history.

According to film historian and author

Charles Higham, RKO-Radio Pictures had purchased the book as a vehicle for Dolores Del Rio in 1932. Eleven years went by without it being made, and independent producer James Cassidy picked it up for next to nothing. He sold it to MGM in 1945 for about $70,000. MGM boss Louis B. Mayer was not satisfied with the eight attempts by as many writers in as many years that he commissioned, but in 1953 the movie was almost made. Alan Jay Lerner wrote a script for Vincente Minnelli to film in South America. Actress Pier Angeli was hired to play the part of Rima, the jungle girl. But a change of command at the studio relegated the movie to the shelf once again, until Ferrer came along and decided it would be a perfect vehicle for his wife.

"He wanted the world to see me as sexy," Audrey recalled with a laugh. "It didn't matter that I was straight as a board, a fine line in bone structure; he thought I had real oomph appeal, and that Rima would bring it out."

Set in Venezuela on the cusp of the twentieth century, *Green Mansions* tells the fantastical love story of Rima (Audrey), an otherworldly creature more at home with birds and deer than with humans, and an explorer, Abel (Anthony Perkins), who tries to revive in her a feeling of womanhood.

"I thought she was the most exquisite creature I'd ever seen," Perkins said, "and I was very nervous to be directed by her husband. What I mean is, I wished she didn't have a husband! I mean there was a lot of kissing and touching and smooching in this movie, it was a charged atmosphere, with the jungle and the animals, and the sense of heat and color, and the last thing I wanted was for somebody's husband to ruin it."

When asked how it felt to have one's husband watch another man embrace her, indeed tell that other man just how it's done, Audrey looked up with her wide eyes and smiled.

"Uninhibited," she replied.

Audrey loved filming the movie, because she developed a strong attachment to one of her costars. The deer that follows her in *Green Mansions*, called "Ip" because of the sound it made, became so close to Audrey that she adopted it. At home, it shared its bed with Mr. Famous.

The public didn't care. They collectively avoided the $3 million movie, and it turned out to be an unmitigated flop at the box office. Like his three previous directorial efforts — *Girl of the Limberlost*, *The Secret Fury*, and *Vendetta* — *Green Mansions* was a blot on Ferrer's record of accomplishments.

Audrey's star, however, continued to rise.

The Nun's Story was nominated for eight Academy Awards, including Best Actress for Audrey. *Films in Review* magazine called her portrait of Sister Luke one of the great performances of the screen. "Miss Hepburn reveals the kind of acting talent that can project inner feelings, of both depth and complexity, so skillfully, you must scrutinize her intently on a second or third viewing of *The Nun's Story* to perceive how she does it," it rhapsodized.

Bosley Crowther of the *New York Times*, who had called Audrey his favorite actress in the whole world, also heralded her performance: "Through the radiant-eyed Miss Hepburn, [*The Nun's Story*] firmly details and reveals the effects of this rigorous education on one sensitive young body and soul . . . In the role of the nun, Miss Hepburn is fluid and luminous. From her eyes and her eloquent expressions emerge a character that is warm and involved."

Though she lost the Academy Award to Simone Signoret for her portrayal of an older woman in love with Laurence Harvey in *Room at the Top*, Audrey won a host of awards for *The Nun's Story*, including the New York Film Critics' Award for 1959.

It was at the gala dinner that someone compared her to the Virgin of Fra Angelico's *An-*

nunciation. Audrey loved the comparison. She knew that the Virgin in any annunciation is without a doubt about to become a mother.

Chapter 19

Immediately before she began work on her first Western, John Huston's *The Unforgiven*, Audrey discovered she was pregnant again.

"Of course, I attributed it to my revelations at the leper colony," Audrey said. "After looking in on an insane asylum, visiting the leper colony and going to Mass there, talking to the missionaries and watching all the doctors and nurses perform so much good, I just felt better, freer. I knew that my lot in life was just as it was meant to be. I had faith that if God wanted me to have a child, I would. When I became pregnant again, I knew He wanted it, too. But I decided to go ahead with the picture because I didn't think it was a good idea for me to sit around, waiting. Neither did Mel. Anytime I sat around for too long, I'd work myself into nervousness. We both thought *The Unforgiven* would be the perfect tonic. And I was thrilled to be working with John Huston."

What Audrey didn't bank on were filming conditions that rivaled those on *The Nun's*

Story for level of discomfort. Huston decided that the story of the rivalry between a pioneer family and the Kiowa Indians in the Texas panhandle of the 1860s would have to be filmed in Mexico, to have the proper primitive look. The fact that his family lived nearby may have also influenced his decision.

She and the rest of the cast — Burt Lancaster, Audie Murphy, and Lillian Gish among them — arrived at the desertlike location after a six-hour trip in a rickety station wagon during which everybody wondered what kind of transportation Huston was taking.

But like Audrey, the rest of the stars were fascinated by Ben Maddow's script for *The Unforgiven*. Ferrer had called it "the thinkingest Western he'd ever read," a line which Audrey adored and shared with her new colleagues.

The story of the rivalry between two ranching families — the Zacharys and the Rawlinses — *The Unforgiven* focuses its plot development on Rachel Zachary (Audrey), the adopted daughter of Mattilda (Lillian Gish) and sister to Ben (Burt Lancaster), Cash (Audie Murphy), and Andy (Doug McClure).

Rachel is revealed to be a full-blooded Kiowa Indian by Abe Kelsey (Joseph Wiseman), who tells a haunting story about her capture. Years ago, he says, his son was kidnapped by the Kiowas. In an act of revenge, Kelsey and the Zachary sire, Will, burned down an Indian village. Rachel was its sole survivor. Will took the baby home and decided to raise it as his own. When the Kiowas offered to trade Kelsey's son for Rachel, the Zacharys refused.

"I loved the melodrama of the story," Audrey recalled. "And I felt that I could easily play someone with Indian roots. But I didn't count on riding quite as much as I did."

Although Huston wanted to focus on the theme of racial intolerance in the movie, United Artists insisted that he make the movie look like a traditional and highly commercial Western. As a result, Audrey spent days on horseback.

"I hadn't ridden since I was a child," Audrey recalled, "and I was petrified, but willing. Somebody had told me I was the highest-paid actress of the year, and I felt the company should get its money's worth."

In fact, Audrey was paid $200,000 for *The Unforgiven*, which did rank her with the Hollywood elite in 1959. But no amount of money could compensate her for her well-being.

She wanted to prove herself to Huston, show that she could do the stunts required of her. She had overheard him compliment her in his offhand way to a visiting reporter

— "She's as good as the other Hepburn," he said, alluding to Katharine, the star of his *African Queen* — and Audrey wanted to prove him right.

She agreed to do all the riding herself, using no stunt doubles. As Huston led her over to the white stallion, Diablo (rumored to have once been the favorite horse of Fulgencio Batista, who had just been ousted as Cuba's leader), she felt herself tighten with fear. But after several hours of practice, riding with and without a saddle, Audrey felt confident that she could film the scene.

But the addition of camera lights upset another horse, which galloped toward Diablo. Diablo bolted toward the lights. A member of the crew threw up his arms to stop the other horse. Instead Diablo stopped short. "I knew I was going to be thrown," Audrey said. "All I could think of was the baby."

By the time Huston and Dr. Felipe Hernandez, a Mexican doctor assigned to the film, arrived at Audrey's side on the cement-hard ground, she was slipping in and out of consciousness.

"Every time she would open her eyes," the doctor recalled, "she would say, 'Please don't tell Mel. Promise that you won't tell Mel. He worries so much.' Frankly, I was extremely worried. I wasn't sure Audrey Hepburn was ever going to walk again. I was afraid she had broken her back."

According to Burt Lancaster, Audrey joked the whole time she was waiting for the stretcher.

"I had to do something to get out of this dump," she said to him. The entire company watched in disbelief.

"Her voice was quavering," Lancaster recalled. "That lovely, soft voice of hers was even more tentative. Every time she tried to put us at ease, that quiet little voice of hers made matters worse. She sounded like she was fading away."

The sedative was taking effect. She was taken by ambulance to the Durango hospital, where Ferrer and her personal physician, Dr. Howard Mendelson, were waiting. They examined her while she slept.

When she finally opened her eyes three hours later, Ferrer knew what she wanted to hear. "The baby's fine," he said, "but the mother's a little battered."

The X-rays showed four broken vertebrae, two sprained ankles, a sprained wrist, and torn muscles in her lower back. After consultation with her doctor, United Artists shut down production on *The Unforgiven* for three weeks, uncertain if the movie would ever be completed.

Audrey was sent to recuperate at a rented Beverly Hills villa. Ironically, Marie-Louise Habets, the former nun whose life had inspired *The Nun's Story*, was in the Los Angeles area and was called in to minister to Audrey.

"I was on my back for twenty days straight, listening to Mel rant and rave about how careless John [Huston] had been. I was his captive audience, and I hated it. I didn't blame anyone, except myself maybe, because I'm sure I conveyed my own fear to the horse. But I certainly wasn't going to allow a picture to be lost because of me. I heard the wait for my recovery cost about two hundred fifty thousand dollars. If they spent that much hoping I'd get better, then I wasn't going to let them down."

Audrey completed the shoot wearing an uncomfortable orthopedic back brace. On the last day of shooting, she had to remount Diablo for some additional footage.

"I held my breath, said my prayers, and just did it," Audrey recalled. "This time, he was as calm as an angel."

When *The Unforgiven* opened, critics found it interesting, but flawed. They commented on its somber tone and its oddly upbeat score by Dmitri Tiomkin. They wondered why one character disappeared without a trace midway through the film. They snickered at a typically

Huston surrealistic scene in which Indians attack a piano (after Mattilda has played some Mozart, presumably to calm the tribe). They questioned the acceptance of incest between Rachel and her adopted brother in the movie.

But they all agreed on Audrey's performance. She grows in the part, they concurred, from a bright, spontaneous young girl to a mature woman, one whose zest for life is tempered by the knowledge of her heritage.

Audrey was finally being reviewed as an actress, not an ingenue. "Some of my pictures I don't care for," Huston said at the time. "This one I actively dislike. But Hepburn was a trouper and I wished I had used her to better advantage. She could have carried the picture if I let her."

But at home, she was still treated like a little girl. Ferrer was still incensed about the riding accident, and he insisted that she return to Burgenstock in the spring of 1959 and rest. In fact, her back was not fully healed, and she needed to take it easy, but still she bridled at the thought of having nothing to do but worry about the baby.

A much-needed distraction came in the form of *No Bail for the Judge*, a mystery written by Henry Cecil and adapted for the screen — with Audrey in mind — by Samuel Taylor.

Its main attraction was its director — Alfred Hitchcock.

"I adored the script that Mr. Hitchcock sent over," Audrey said. "I'll never forget the story. I was to play a barrister in London. My father, a judge at the Old Bailey, is wrongly accused of murdering a prostitute and I was supposed to defend him. I hire a crook to help gather evidence, and the crook was to be played by Laurence Harvey. I was so excited, I told Mr. Hitchcock to send over the contracts."

A day later, she fell ill while knitting a pair of booties and two hours later, miscarried her baby. She was at the beginning of her third trimester. She backed out of the movie, Hitchcock decided to cancel rather than recast, and he never forgave her. It was yet another example of Hitchcock's heavy-handed treatment of his stars, especially the leading actresses of his movies. He was notorious for mentally tormenting them.

"All the emotional strides I thought I'd made, all the growth and the lifting of the depression, were gone the moment the doctor told me I'd lost another baby," Audrey said quietly. "I was angry. I blamed God. I blamed myself. I blamed John Huston. I blamed Mel for not protecting me. I was one bundle of anger and recriminations. I felt like hell. I looked like hell. And I didn't care."

She began smoking two to three packs of cigarettes a day, and again refused to eat. Her mother was flown in from London to try to persuade Audrey to try to get well, but even the Baroness had no influence this time. Despite their dislike for one another, Audrey's mother and her husband joined forces and considered committing her to a mental institution, but neither one could actually bear the thought. It became too emotionally draining for the Baroness when she realized she could do nothing to improve Audrey's spirits, so after three weeks, she left.

Of course, Ferrer did his best to keep his wife's condition a secret, and living in Switzerland, he was able to keep a lid on the rumors. But Audrey was unable to return to work, and there were whispers in Hollywood that she was gravely ill with a mysterious disease she had picked up in Mexico. In truth, she was gravely ill — with depression, and was forced to turn down a whole raft of movie offers. She passed on *Cleopatra*, the movie that gave Elizabeth Taylor a $1 million contract as well as another chance at love, this time with Richard Burton. She declined Otto Preminger's *The Cardinal* (the role eventually going to Carol Lynley) and, more significantly, *West Side Story* (the Maria character, which went to Natalie Wood). She also passed on *A Taste of Honey* (Rita Tushingham), *In the Cool of the Day* (Jane Fonda), and *Hawaii* (Julie Andrews).

"My heart was broken and so was Mel's," she said about that bleak time. "For months, we didn't talk much. But he took complete care of me. Keeping so busy, I'm sure, helped him get better. And just seeing him more chipper lifted my spirits."

In early summer of 1959, just seven months after her miscarriage, Audrey became pregnant again. "I told no one except for Mel," she said. "I tried not to even think of it myself. I was afraid I was somehow a jinx. I made pacts with God. I made wild promises that I knew I could never keep. But I would have done anything at all to insure this baby's well-being, and for several months, I refused to get out of bed at all."

She did accompany Ferrer to Italy and France, where he costarred in two supernatural thrillers — *Blood and Roses* and *The Hands of Orlac* — but she rarely left her hotel rooms, preferring instead to sit quietly and wait.

When she returned to Burgenstock, her doctor advised her to go for long walks to help strengthen the muscles she had so severely injured on the set of *The Unforgiven*. Both her personal physician and her obstetrician were concerned that she was too weak and too small for an easy delivery.

"Once I was told I had to have some exercise," Audrey recalled, "I reveled in it. The air felt great. It truly lifted my spirits. Anytime one of my black moods starts to descend, I try to remember how much exercise helps." She also surrounded herself with children, hoping their laughter could be heard by her baby.

On January 17, 1960, at Lucerne's Municipal Maternity Clinic, Audrey gave birth to a 9 $1/2$-pound baby boy. The labor was arduous, but Audrey maintains she really didn't feel the pain.

"I was so excited by the occasion, the miracle of giving birth, that everything that was going on felt right. I remember hearing a lot of clapping — I discovered later there was a tremendous storm going on while I was in the delivery room — and I just felt the world was applauding my efforts. It felt better than any performance I'd ever given. It *was* better. I had waited my whole life for the moment of giving birth, and it finally happened. I'm sure it's great when you're eighteen, but I was thirty and the long wait made it that much sweeter."

As obsessed as Audrey had been with Ferrer when she first married him, she became equally possessed by her son, not leaving his side once during his first three months. In light of her celebrity, she was tremendously worried about the safety of the baby and particularly concerned about kidnapping.

The christening of Sean Ferrer (his name means "gift of God") took place in the same church where his parents were married.

His godparents were Audrey's half brother Jan, who had recently taken a job as an executive with Shell Oil in Southeast Asia, and Ferrer's sister Terry. After the service, Terry expressed some odd concerns to Henry Taylor, Jr., the American ambassador to Switzerland and one of the few guests outside of family members at the service.

"Audrey talked about how she was trying to include her dog Famous in the activities surrounding the new baby. She didn't want him to feel left out. But there was no mention of her husband."

Their marriage had suffered irreparable damage due to Audrey's recurrent depression over her miscarriages. Sadly, by the time their first child was born, they were both secretly considering divorce.

Chapter 20

Neither mother nor father did much else but gawk at Sean during the first six months of his life. Audrey and Ferrer had waited so long for the birth of their baby — six years — that their enthusiasm was fully understood and accepted. But they were practical people, too. Audrey wanted to get back to work to earn some money.

"On the surface, Mel kept saying it would be a good idea to do a movie to give the baby a little breathing space, but I think he was worried about finances, too. My earning power was higher than his at that time, and I think it hurt his pride tremendously. That was one area that we never discussed. But when the script for *Breakfast at Tiffany's* was floated by, Mel was very enthusiastic."

The plot of the movie differs considerably from the Truman Capote novella upon which it is based, but the spirit of the work remains buoyantly the same.

Holly Golightly, formerly Lulamae Barnes from the backwoods of Texas, lives in a Manhattan brownstone on the Upper East Side. A party girl, she earns enough money to keep herself in cottage cheese and little black dresses by accepting fifty-dollar "donations" from her dates whenever she goes to the powder room.

She also earns a "salary" of a hundred dollars a week by visiting gangster Sally Tomato (Alan Reed) at Sing Sing.

George Peppard portrayed Holly's new neighbor and paramour Paul Varjak in the movie, and Audrey was delighted to finally have a leading man close to her age. "But his style of acting unnerved me," she recalled. "He was from 'The Method' school, and I felt very inadequate just going on my instincts while George would have thought-out reasons for what he was doing."

As usual, Audrey had other doubts about the project as well. In this instance, they were justified. By nature, she was a quiet, introspective woman who preferred to be surrounded by animals than by people. And Holly Golightly, Capote's most memorably kooky character, defined the word "extrovert." She was the epitome of "outgoing." She lived and breathed for and through other people. She fed off them. They gave her effervescence, much like the champagne she so loved. "I was nothing like her," Audrey said, "but I felt I could 'act' Holly. That was a revolutionary thought for me. After so many movies, I no longer felt like an amateur. I knew I would always be able to learn something, but I finally realized I could give something as well. I knew the part would be a challenge, but I wanted it anyway."

Again, the practical side of Audrey also showed through. She wanted to boost her effort to change her image from young girl to worldly woman. Holly Golightly would push her over the top. Here was a character from contemporary fiction whom intellectuals analyzed and secretaries imitated. After portraying her, Audrey hoped she could quiet the voices who spoke of her virginal innocence. She knew those voices, however honest, would doom her career; she wouldn't be able to work again. There weren't too many roles requiring a middle-aged woman dripping with purity.

All that made Holly Golightly, a character who says, "I'm used to being the top banana in the shock department," even more appealing.

After much discussion, Paramount persuaded her to leave Sean in Switzerland with his nanny. The studio felt the baby might distract Audrey, as well as hinder her screen image as a swinging party girl.

She and Ferrer flew to New York and while

she worked on *Breakfast at Tiffany's*, he tried to drum up more screenplays that would promote the newly minted image of his wife as a full-fledged woman. His own career was flagging, and to prevent depression, he plunged into organizing his wife's life.

Meanwhile, Audrey fought her own demons of insecurity. "Manhattan was a rude awakening," she recalled. "I hadn't been back for any extended period of time for so long, and it seemed more crowded than ever, just teeming with people. They scared me."

But like her character, she hid her fear. "There's this speech that George Peppard delivers to me in the movie that I'm convinced was meant specifically for me."

In the movie, Peppard, as suitor Paul Varjak, eventually tells her off.

"Do you know what's wrong with you, Miss Whoever-You-Are?" he says, his anger building. "You're chicken. You got no guts. You're afraid to stick out your chin and say, 'Okay, life's a fact. People do fall in love. People do belong to each other because that's the only chance anybody's got for real happiness.' You call yourself a free spirit, a wild thing, and you're terrified somebody's going to stick you in a cage. Well, baby, you're already in that cage. You built it for yourself, and it's not bound on the west by Tulip, Texas, or on the east by Somaliland. It's wherever you go because no matter where you run, you just end up running into yourself."

If Audrey was able to pull off her portrayal of Holly Golightly — and the critics were mixed in their assessment — it is because she identified with her character's vulnerabilities.

Despite the fact that she was at the height of her popularity, cinematographer Franz Planer, who had worked on so many of Audrey's movies, said that she was never as insecure as she was during this movie.

"She wanted to look stunning," Planer recalled, "and she did, but she did not look like Marilyn Monroe, whom she had heard Capote modeled Holly after. She would confide in me, and I did everything in my power to persuade her that she was just perfect, but she knew that wasn't the case."

The day Audrey filmed the famous scene outside of Tiffany's was particularly difficult. Again she felt much like the words her character uttered.

"The blues," says Holly Golightly, "are because you are getting fat or maybe it's been raining too long. You're just sad, that's all. The 'mean reds' are horrible. Suddenly you're afraid, and you don't even know what you're afraid of. Did you ever get that feeling? . . . Well, when I get it, the only thing that does any good is to jump into a cab and go to Tiffany's. Calms me down right away. The quietness and the proud look of it. Nothing very bad can happen to you there."

In fact, Audrey thought she might be mobbed to death the morning she filmed the famous scene. Forty security guards and hundreds of New York City cops surrounded her that day as she gazed longingly into the front display window, munching a Danish (which she detested) and drinking a cup of coffee in a humble paper cup.

But that paper cup, insisted director Blake Edwards, was the symbol of Holly's humble roots. Edwards, who was eager to change his reputation as a competent director of television series to that of a renowned director of movie comedies, still would not compromise the poignancy of the film to get a few laughs.

"The movie is a hybrid," he said. "It was meant to be. I'd like to think that just as soon as you laugh, you might well up at the next line." That was certainly the case after listening to Audrey sing "Moon River" in the movie.

Edwards had composer Henry Mancini and lyricist Johnny Mercer write the song especially for Audrey. Like Givenchy, who again designed stunningly simple dresses for Audrey to wear, Mancini was inspired by her look of vulnerability. "I kind of knew what to write, at least what track I should be on, by reading the script," he said. "And Audrey's big eyes gave me the push to get a little more sentimental than I usually do. Those eyes of hers could carry it. I knew that.

" 'Moon River' was written for her," Mancini continued. "No one else has ever understood it so completely. There have been more than one thousand versions of 'Moon River,' but hers is unquestionably the greatest. When we previewed the film, the head of Paramount was there, and he said, 'One thing's for sure: That fucking song's gotta go.' Audrey shot right up out of her chair! Mel Ferrer had to put his hand on her arm to restrain her. That's the closest I had ever seen her come to losing control."

Despite the fact that Audrey "crossed her heart and kissed her elbow," something that Holly did when she needed good luck, the movie was not the stellar success for which she'd hoped. The critics liked it, and they liked her, but there were no rave reviews.

"I always wonder if I risked enough on that one," she mused a few months before her death. "I should have been a little more outrageous. But at the time, as a new mother, I was about as wild as I could be. If only I were a Method player, huh? But the fact is,

I didn't really believe in The Method. I believed more in good casting. And I'm still not sure about Holly and me . . ."

But others were not so ambivalent. In time, critics began to fully appreciate her efforts as Holly. Shortly before she died, David Thompson wrote in *American Film* magazine about *Breakfast at Tiffany's*. "For Audrey-philes, this is at the top of the heap," he said, "a true star vehicle that allows her to be kooky, dramatic, winsome, tragic, and breathtakingly beautiful."

Other retrospective opinions bore out the belief that the movie was a charming period piece that owed its major appeal to Audrey. In her obituary in the *New York Times*, critic Caryn James wrote that Audrey was "justly acclaimed" as Holly Golightly.

But it was the members of the fashion industry who truly appreciated Audrey's contribution in *Breakfast at Tiffany's*. "The devil-may-care attitude she displayed as Holly Golightly in *Breakfast at Tiffany's* made her an icon that will live forever," said designer Marc Jacobs. "In the movie, Audrey is the personification of sophisticated, simple, useful spontaneity."

Chapter 21

In 1960, Audrey was voted among the most popular actresses alive, sharing the honor with Elizabeth Taylor, Marilyn Monroe, Doris Day, and Shirley MacLaine. But the adulation had its drawbacks.

"A young man started to follow me," she revealed. "From New York to Switzerland, and anytime I went anywhere, it seems. In the beginning, I thought I was imagining things, or exaggerating in my mind the number of times I would see him. I didn't tell anyone for a long time, for two reasons I guess. First, I felt if I kept it quiet, he might just go away, and second, I didn't want to anger him. It seemed to me if he was spending so much time on my trail, he must really be crazy. I was deathly afraid, but I kept it to myself. I had this reputation as a delicate creature, which I didn't mind, as long as it wasn't based on real facts. I mean, it would not do me well to have people think I was a genuine bundle of nerves. Which I was a lot of the time!"

That's why when the next project came up, Audrey surprised everyone by jumping at the chance to play Karen Wright, a woman whose reputation is ruined by gossip and slander, in *The Children's Hour*.

The screen version of Lillian Hellman's play also stars Shirley MacLaine as Wright's close friend and teaching colleague, Martha Dobie, accused by a young student of having a lesbian relationship with Wright. James Garner portrays Audrey's beau, who breaks off their engagement after he begins to believe the rumors about her.

Directed by William Wyler, who oversaw Audrey's momentous Hollywood debut in *Roman Holiday*, *The Children's Hour* was Audrey's first psychological drama.

"I liked to try new forms," she said. "But I never went out on a limb too far. I felt safe here because I knew Wyler so well and, of course, he had directed the first film version of *The Children's Hour* [*These Three*, in 1936, starring Merle Oberon and Miriam Hopkins], so I felt he knew the material inside and out."

Because of the secret stalker, Audrey was extremely wary of strangers when she arrived in Los Angeles to begin filming, and journalists pegged her as uncooperative and aloof. She didn't allow them to visit the Coldwater Canyon house she had rented for herself,

Ferrer, Sean, and Sean's nanny, because she didn't want her address to leak out.

On the set, she experienced further difficulties in working with MacLaine. "When we first met," Audrey recalled, "I think it's safe to say we didn't like one another at all. I bet we despised one another! I of course kept that to myself, because that was my style. In fact, I think that's what went wrong with the two of us at the beginning: We had wildly different styles. As soon as I let down my guard, I fell in love with Shirley. That's the wrong phrasing for this movie, but I did enjoy her antics. She helped me through a very hard time, and she didn't even know it."

Because she was so afraid of her mysterious follower, Audrey brought Sean with her to the set every day. She also carted along Famous, as if the boy and the dog were actually brothers.

Before one of the most important scenes in the movie, when the malicious young student eavesdrops on her teachers and then tattles on them, the dog escaped from Audrey's dressing room.

"In my own way — and full of the denial I'm famous for — I felt with Famous there and Sean, I was keeping it all together, I could somehow keep out the bad guys. But when my doggy ran away, everything fell apart. I had to stop filming that day. Wyler was furious. Shirley just thought I was my sensitive self. Nobody knew that I'd been dealing with this intermittent intruder who seemed to be getting closer and closer."

Like *The Children's Hour*, in which the word "lesbian" is never spoken, Audrey kept to herself what was actually bothering her.

Famous was sighted later in the day on a high wall in the back lot of the studio. When Audrey saw him, she hushed the knot of crew members gathered to look for him, and climbed the wall herself to retrieve him.

He was safe, and because of that, so was she. For the time being, at least.

About a week later, on Wilshire Boulevard, her precious Famous was hit by a speeding car and killed. The driver was never found.

"In the back of my mind, I was sure the accident had something to do with the man who was following me, but I tried not to think about it," she said.

She returned to Europe with her family, and rarely left her home in Burgenstock.

There, Audrey obsessed about the poor notices for *The Children's Hour*. Brooks Atkinson of the *New York Times* called it "lugubrious," "sensational," and "turgid." "Instead of being wowed by an off-beat combination," wrote Archer Winsten in the *New York Post*, "we get a pair of off-hand performances in a sentimental slob of a film."

Ferrer was getting tired of her fears, which he felt she exaggerated to gain attention and sympathy. He left her alone in Switzerland and flew to Spain to begin a small role in a project of his own he'd been pinning his latest hopes on, *The Fall of the Roman Empire*.

While he was away, B actor-turned-director Richard Quine, perhaps best known for *My Sister Eileen*, and several other early Jack Lemmon movies, visited Audrey in Burgenstock and stayed at the new guest house Fritz Frey had recently built for her. He had heard that she wanted to take a break from films, and decided he would have a better chance in person of persuading her to star in *Paris When It Sizzles*.

The story of a broken-down screenwriter who encourages his lovely secretary to help him act out his stories, the screenplay — written by *Breakfast at Tiffany's* George Axelrod — was based on Julien Duvivier's movie *La Fête Henriette*.

"Richard was so sweet," Audrey said. "He told me how perfect I'd be for the part. After not feeling so perfect for either of my last two films, his words sounded good. I liked the idea of doing something light, and I liked even more making the decision myself."

There was one major complication, however. William Holden had already been cast in the part of the aging screenwriter. Having heard about their onetime dalliance, Quine wasn't sure how Audrey would respond to the news.

"I was delighted," she said. "I didn't show it, but the fact that Bill was in the movie clinched it for me. I hadn't seen him for about ten years. In fact, I think the last time we even said anything to one another was when I introduced him to Mel, who was my fiancé at the time, at some nightclub in New York."

Holden had not fared well during their years apart. He was still in love with Audrey, and he escaped from his pain by drinking. By the time the movie began, he was an undeniable alcoholic.

"I wasn't fully aware of how bad his drinking had become," Audrey said. "I was used to hard-drinking actors, and I just didn't realize that Bill had stepped over the line. I would have said something if I did."

Instead, Audrey encouraged Holden's attentions, hoping to breathe a little life into her own marriage. Yet when Ferrer read reports of his wife being seen on the town with Holden, he quelled all rumors, telling people they were just old friends.

On the set, the mood was tense. Holden

would often arrive drunk. Yet he'd insist upon working, trying to prove he was man enough to get through anything. Audrey, on the other hand, was going through a period of over-whelming insecurity, a classic mid-life crisis, fearful that Ferrer was losing interest. She became so unsure of herself, she began to believe she was really ugly and insisted that renowned cinematographer Claude Renoir be fired because he wasn't able to compensate for her flaws on camera.

Noël Coward and Marlene Dietrich were invited to do cameo bits, as was Ferrer, whom Quine hoped could calm his wife. Instead, he made matters worse, exacerbating her insecurities by not overloading her with affection.

"This was without a doubt the worst film experience of my career," Audrey admitted. "It was as if we all let our worst instincts get the best of us. I realize now I was being manipulative with Bill, that I needed him to pay attention to me to boost my ego. But he was being pathetic, really, and angry, and Richard Quine couldn't control either of us. Though he did try, poor man. He moved next door to Bill just to keep a lid on his drinking. But it didn't work. Bill would invariably outsmart him and then show up under my window, serenading like a hyena. He bought this sporty Ferrari during the shoot and I was always petrified he was going to smash it up."

After Holden's wife arrived on the set, she persuaded him to go to a rehabilitative center for a short stay. Filming was suspended while he underwent treatment for alcoholism.

Audrey's mood improved considerably — and with it the rest of the cast's — when she received word from Burgenstock that a twenty-two-year-old science student, Jean-Claude Thouroude, had turned himself in for breaking and entering her home.

"He had moved to Switzerland to be near me," she said. "He had stolen my Oscar for *Roman Holiday*, but I didn't know it. He had written so many fan letters that my secretaries had stopped answering him. When he went to the police station, he told them he was in love with me, and if I only could meet him, I would be in love with him, too.

"I was so very relieved that he gave himself up. It's a terrible feeling to sense you're being followed, without really being certain. A big weight lifted off my shoulders. I felt I could breathe again."

Audrey was so buoyant she decided to stay in Paris for several more months, extending the lease on the Bourbon château on the road to Fontainebleau she had rented for herself and Sean. "It's funny — the house was extremely secure, with a locked gate and high walls surrounding it," she recalled. "But I never felt safe in it until after they caught that man who followed me. After that, I felt it was impenetrable."

It was this newfound sense of security which encouraged Audrey to accept her next offer from Stanley Donen: to play a cool, calm, unflappable character, completely unlike herself, in *Charade*.

A stylish romantic mystery that perfectly showcased Audrey's charms, *Charade* tells the story of a young widow, Reggie Lambert (Audrey), who tries to make sense of her husband's life after his death and a convoluted series of events lead her to believe he may have been a crook. Cary Grant and Walter Matthau aid her in her quest, and the marvelous cast also includes James Coburn and George Kennedy.

"I wouldn't have done the movie without Cary or Audrey," said director Donen. "And they felt the same way, even though they hadn't acted together before. When I showed the script to Cary, he looked at me wistfully and said, 'It could be great, if only we could get Audrey for Reggie.' She said the same thing about his part. Uncanny! Although I had always talked each of them up to the other, until I saw them on-screen together in the first dailies, I really didn't know how right

I was. The chemistry was organic — it just was. I have never had so confident a feeling about a movie as I did about *Charade* after the first day of shooting."

A comedy as well as a thriller, Peter Stone's intelligent, witty screenplay manages to depict the development of a believable romance between Audrey and Cary without a single kiss being exchanged. But the innuendoes tickled. "How do you shave in there?" Audrey asks, pointing to the famous cleft in Grant's chin.

"Cary was extremely sensitive about our age difference," Audrey said. "I think he was fifty-eight when we got started, and I was thirty-three. But I had often played younger than my years, and he was afraid he'd be accused of cradle snatching if we had a full-blown romance. He just had this innate sense of good taste. Peter Stone was wonderful about it. He changed his script — and each word of it was marvelous — to reflect Gary's concerns. He made it even funnier. I remember one line he added. Gary says to me, 'At my age, who wants to hear the word *serious?*' And I was always chasing him, don't forget. I chased him around Europe in that movie."

What the movie lacked in plausibility, it made up for in charm. When it was released in 1964, critics and audiences alike adored it. "A debonair, macabre thriller — romantic, scary, satisfying," wrote Pauline Kael. "If Hitchcock could only laugh at himself, this is the movie he'd make," said Rex Reed.

Paris When It Sizzles, on the other hand, fizzled when it opened. "All I could think about when I saw it was how crooked my teeth looked," Audrey said. "They are the same teeth in *Charade*, but I didn't notice anything wrong with them there!"

Chapter 22

On November 22, 1963, Audrey had just finished recording "Wouldn't It Be Loverly" from *My Fair Lady* when director George Cukor abruptly pulled her aside.

"JFK's been shot," he said. "The president's gone."

As in all times of true emotional devastation, Audrey was stronger than people expected her to be. When Cukor could not get the words out, it was she who took his place at the jerry-rigged podium and borrowed a bullhorn from one of the sound engineers. "The president of the United States is dead," she told the stunned workers. "All we know is that he has been shot in Dallas. I think we should have two minutes of silence to pray or do whatever you feel is appropriate."

After she announced the news, she provided a shoulder to lean on for all the shocked cast and crew members of *My Fair Lady*. "May he rest in peace," she told them. They wanted to take the rest of the day off, but Jack Warner, the head of the studio, insisted that they continue working. *My Fair Lady* had been in trouble for weeks, he reasoned, and despite the pain of the news, they all had to keep going. Audrey went along with the decision, but to help herself do so she tried to remember a time when she had really wanted to go to work on *My Fair Lady*.

It was before she'd even begun. The day the call had come from her agent, Kurt Frings, telling her to sit down, she'd won the part, was the happiest moment of her career.

"I was in Burgenstock and the connection was so poor," she said. "I had a hard time hearing Kurt. And he usually was such a booming man. '*My Fair Lady* is all yours,' he kept repeating. When I finally got it, I whooped. Mother was upstairs showering and she rushed down covered in a towel, thinking something awful had happened. Well, little did she know it, or I know it, but she was right!"

Based on George Bernard Shaw's *Pygmalion*, Alan Jay Lerner and Frederick Loewe's *My Fair Lady* was the hit of the 1956 Broadway season when Jack Warner started negotiating for screen rights. The wrangling took nearly five years and cost $5.5 million — at the time, the most expensive screen rights in the history of the movies.

From the beginning of its run, and despite

her rave reviews, there were rumors that the studio would not ask newcomer Julie Andrews to reprise her role as Eliza Doolittle, the cockney flower girl who is taught to behave like a duchess. It was not that Jack Warner didn't think she was supremely talented, but after spending $5.5 million, he wanted a star with marquee value.

Kurt Frings closely followed the negotiations. Audrey had never asked him for anything except the starring role in *My Fair Lady*. The large, loud, tough, German-accented agent, who at times also represented Elizabeth Taylor, Lucille Ball, Brigitte Bardot, and Cary Grant, would do anything to please his Audrey. He pounced when the time was right and he landed not only the role of a lifetime for Audrey, but a $1-million-plus contract to go with it.

Warner was far from sold on Rex Harrison (who starred in the play on Broadway) for the role of Professor Henry Higgins, the curmudgeonly phonetics expert who drills Eliza in pronunciation to win a bet. Laurence Olivier's name came up, as did Rock Hudson's and Cary Grant's. But Grant told Warner the role belonged to Harrison, and the studio head actually listened to him.

In May of 1963, Audrey arrived in Hollywood ready to conquer the film. She, Ferrer,

Sean, and Sean's nanny checked into the Beverly Hills Hotel and two days later rented a stately white-columned mansion in Bel Air.

"Everything was so rushed from the moment I arrived," she recalled. "I had just finished unpacking in the hotel — my candlesticks and framed photos and such — when Mel walked in with the news that a house had been found for us! Never did we find one so fast. We moved out of the hotel, I unpacked all over again, and that afternoon, the big shots came to call."

Director Cukor arrived at Audrey's home with Alan Jay Lerner and costume designer Cecil Beaton.

"It was all very friendly on the surface," she continued, "but I knew they were looking me over, and it made me very self-conscious. I felt like a piece of property. But I did get along famously with Cecil. I was so nervous about working with someone other than Givenchy on such an important movie, but Cecil put me completely at ease. He was a lot of fun — a schoolboy imp, really."

Audrey's main concern was extracting a promise that her voice would be used in the movie. She was adamant about wanting to do her own singing, and felt that her guests were on her side.

"There was some mention of mixing my

voice with another voice, like what they did for Leslie Caron in *Gigi*, and I was fine with that. Look, I would have been fine with whatever they decided, as long as they were honest about it. I was under the impression that I would be doing most of the singing, so I worked night and day to improve my voice."

She worked twelve to fourteen hours a day rehearsing, from early June until shooting began in August. "I had singing lessons all morning with Susan Seton. In the late afternoons, I would have an hour of diction, trying to get the cockney accent down with a professor from the University of California [Peter Ladefoged]. There were dancing lessons with Hermes Pan. Work with André Previn. Constant fittings with Cecil. And of course, learning my lines."

By the time shooting began, she had every line down pat, even if she was a little stiff in her delivery. Rex Harrison, however, who had played the part millions of times, could not remember his lines. His problems only added to Audrey's frustration.

"I was having a devilish time with the guttersnipe stuff," she recalled. "I never could get the intonation quite right. It has nothing to do with some innate aristocratic air, as some silly critics once said. I think it's because I learned English from my father at a very young age, and his was perfect. He made a big to-do about speaking correctly, and every time I dropped an *h,* I would stop myself and think of him."

The stress of wanting to give the performance of her career was overwhelming Audrey. "I knew myself very well, and I knew the kind of pressure I worked best under was the self-imposed kind. When everybody else thought I was great, that it was going to be a piece of cake, I disciplined myself to give more, do better. But when people were unsure of me, I often fell apart. That's what I felt like on *My Fair Lady.* I needed their confidence first before I could find my own. And I got the distinct impression everybody had grave doubts about me."

According to an assistant to Alan Jay Lerner, he had been devastated when Julie Andrews was passed over for the role, and he took out his disappointment on Audrey, virtually ignoring her for the whole shoot. In addition, he knew from the start that Marni Nixon had been hired to dub Audrey's singing voice, but he never let Audrey know.

That task was left up to audio music director Ray Heindorf. "I was angry that she had been left in the dark for so long," he said. "I'd watch her in the sound booth, going over and over a phrase. She was so intent. You could see her straining to make it perfect. It killed me. I asked them to tell her about Marni for so long. When I finally got the go-ahead, as difficult as it was, I felt relieved."

Audrey was crushed. She had worked so hard and so long, often rising at 5:30 A.M. to get an extra hour of practice. She knew her voice was not as strong as a professional singer's, but she had sung the whole score to selected members of the cast and crew, including director Cukor, and they had praised her efforts. The duplicity of keeping Nixon's involvement a secret is what bothered her most.

"In looking back," she said, "I can see everybody was trying to protect my feelings from being hurt. Nobody thought I could take the news that my voice wasn't strong enough. Well, I'll tell you, that would have hurt for an hour, but what they did hurt for much longer. I felt used. And I was angry. I was really angry. But I didn't show it outright. I just kept it inside and became more and more difficult on the set."

Audrey demanded that every cast and crew member completely avoid eye contact with her while she was working. She wanted to be in her own little world. She forbade still photographers from being on the set. Several times, she would stop a scene before Cukor yelled "cut" and cry to herself about how impossible the role was. Black scrims were set up throughout Warner's soundstage twelve, where the majority of filming took place, and crew members were asked to crouch behind them every time Cukor yelled "roll 'em." The makeup artists and hairdressers cringed when Audrey appeared each morning because she was so demanding about how she looked. Alberto di Rossi, the artist who devised the special kohl-heavy eye makeup that made her eyes appear to be two dark crystals, found her perfectionism on *My Fair Lady* nearly impossible. "I'd worked with her for years," he recalled, "but this time, nothing we did was ever right. I think she felt insecure about the part, and thought if she looked exactly right, that might compensate for her fears about pulling it off."

The only person involved in *My Fair Lady* with whom she developed a real rapport was Cecil Beaton. "I trusted him completely," Audrey said. "He worked extremely long hours to insure the authenticity of the costumes and to also make sure, in the second half, that they were beautiful on me. A lot of beautiful clothing does not look so beautiful on me, and Cecil's eye was impeccable in gauging what would and would not work. He helped me get over my fear of looking too ugly in the early scenes, too. I remember crying when I first put on that ratty old coat for the flower girl scenes. I felt they were going a little overboard with the dirt-and-grime bit, but Cecil persuaded me the worse I looked in the first scenes, the more dramatic the transformation would be. Of course, he was right."

But no matter how seamless the whole movie looked when it was finished, no matter how many audiences it delighted around the world, Audrey never got over the anguish she felt in making *My Fair Lady*.

"You know that expression, 'Don't wish for something too long, you might get it'? Well, that's how I feel about *My Fair Lady*. I wanted it so much, and afterward, I felt it was cursed."

Perhaps only she was. At the Academy Awards ceremony that year, Audrey was the only principal actor from *My Fair Lady* who was not nominated for an Oscar.

"I wrote my first and only fan letter to her when she was in *Ondine* on Broadway," recalled the singer Eddie Fisher. "I loved her dearly. I was her biggest fan. Once, I happened to have a room next to hers at the Pierre Hotel in New York City. I was having a rough time, and she sat up with me and talked the whole night.

"Years later, when she wasn't even nominated for *My Fair Lady*, I wanted to shoot every member of the Academy for hurting her feelings. I saw her at a dinner parry, and she came over to me with tears in her eyes and asked, 'Are you still my number one fan?' 'Of course I am,' I said. 'I always will be.' She was just too precious to hurt."

"There was a lot of speculation that I wanted to keep Marni Nixon's involvement in the movie a secret," Audrey said. "Nothing of the sort. For the longest time, I didn't know what her involvement was. Then I think somebody told me my voice would be heard about half the time, but it would be blended with Marni's. I told that to some reporter, who conveniently left out the blended part. Then it turned out her voice was used for almost all the singing. Well, it looked like I wanted to deny her her due. Nothing like that at all. But the backlash was incredible."

On April 5, 1965, Audrey screwed up her courage and attended the Academy Awards at the Santa Monica Civil Auditorium, on the arm of George Cukor. Mel was so angry at the Academy for overlooking his wife — and so fed up with having had to placate her for a year as a result — that he refused to go to the ceremony.

At the last minute, Audrey had been asked to present the award for best actor, in place of Patricia Neal, who had suffered a recent stroke and was unable to attend.

"It was a wonderful stroke of luck that I got to give Rex Harrison the Oscar for *My Fair Lady*," she recalled. "He was so grateful, and so gentlemanly. Of course, Julie Andrews was in the audience, and she had done it so brilliantly onstage with him. He looked a little flustered. He looked at me and then at her and said, 'Deep love to, uhm, well, two fair ladies!' Then he quietly offered to cut it in half and share it with me."

It was quite a night for *My Fair Lady*. Prior to Harrison's win, George Cukor had been honored as the top director, Harry Stradling as best cinematographer, Gene Allen and Cecil Beaton for art direction, set decoration, and costumes, George Groves for sound, and André Previn for adaptation of a score.

"Right before the Best Picture award was announced, and right after I had given Rex his statue, came the Best Actress award. Julie Andrews won for *Mary Poppins*. I was delighted for her. I really was. But everybody else was even more thrilled. I think the world perceived her win as some sort of divine justice, and I think I wasn't nominated because they wanted to punish me because she didn't get the part. I realized something then, that it's always better to be thought of as the underdog, and never the winner. The thing is,

I always felt like the underdog. For my whole career, I felt like the underdog."

That year, the world perceived her far differently: as a big star who stepped on her lesser colleagues. The day after the Oscars, Patricia Neal's husband, Roald Dahl, publicly blasted Audrey for not mentioning that she was taking his wife's place at the awards ceremony. "She ignored Pat," he fumed. "Audrey acted as if my wife never existed." Newspapers played up the story as yet another Audrey snub. Even Jack Warner, the man who had hired her for *My Fair Lady*, rebuffed her. When the press asked him who he had voted for as best actress, he said, "Julie Andrews. Who else?"

"I couldn't do anything right that year," she recalled. "I'd even lost my wedding ring."

And she didn't replace it immediately, either.

Chapter 23

Audrey's marriage was in serious trouble. Cast and crew members on *My Fair Lady* recall hearing loud arguments emanating from Audrey's dressing room whenever Ferrer came to visit, but Audrey's publicist, the consummate professional Henry Rogers, was able to keep reports about their difficulties completely out of the papers.

"I was lucky in that regard," Audrey recalled. "Some actresses were always being written up for some transgression or other. Poor Elizabeth [Taylor]! She was portrayed as a man-eater. They didn't go after me quite the same way. Maybe it was my image or something, but they seemed to want to believe in the fairy tale of my life with Mel as much as I did."

The fairy tale, however, was crumbling.

Ferrer felt Audrey should make it her business to do interviews and pose for photos to offset the impression that she was aloof. But after her treatment over *My Fair Lady*, the last thing she wanted to do was submit to more humiliation from the press.

In general, Ferrer felt she was being too submissive about her career. He encouraged her to confront Hubert de Givenchy over his use of her photos to promote Eau de Givenchy, a new line of perfume inspired by Audrey. He thought she should make herself more accessible to the public and tried to persuade her to attend the opening of the Cannes Film Festival in 1965.

"It got very ugly," Audrey recalled. "Mel kept coming up with all these ideas that I just hated. I mean, I would never ask Hubert for money. He was my friend. If I could help him in his business in any way, I would. That's just the way I am. I don't have lots of friends, but the ones I do have last forever, and I would do anything for them. I think it's the same way with them. But Mel and I were at loggerheads. Sadly, my publicist got caught in the crossfire. Mel would tell him one thing, I another, and he didn't know what to do. But when he made some overtures about getting me a special award in order for me to attend Cannes, I balked. The whole thing was out of hand. I fired the poor man. It wasn't his fault at all, but I didn't even want to go to Cannes in the first place."

Instead of working on her career, Audrey dedicated herself to saving her marriage. She traveled with Ferrer on location for a series of his forgettable movies, hoping that constant togetherness might mend their rifts. These small-budget European productions, not one of which would be released in the United States, had none of the amenities she was used to in making Hollywood movies.

"I knew then that Mel and I probably couldn't make it work. My success was killing us. I was a good sport on the locations — making beds, cooking meals; there was no extra money for anything. But he probably felt he wasn't providing for me in the manner to which I'd grown accustomed, and he felt less a man because of it. He had spent the last couple of years in a sort of Mr. Hepburn role, and he was not well suited to taking second place. I admire him for being not well suited. He was his own man. But my success was eating away at what the two of us had together. I just didn't want to admit it."

Audrey returned to Switzerland after traveling on and off with Mel for nearly a year, determined to find a new residence in the French-influenced part of Switzerland so that Sean wouldn't have to attend a German school in Burgenstock.

The village of Tolochenaz, above Lake of Geneva and a half-hour drive from Lausanne, where she found her house, typified her desire for a normal life. A bourgeois hamlet, it was populated primarily by farmers who tended orchards and vineyards.

"It was exactly what I wanted," Audrey said about La Paisible ("The Peaceful Place"), the two-story, eighteenth-century farmhouse of pinkish stone. "It looked rooted and strong and there was not a pretentious beam in its body. When we were looking it over, Assam of Assam [the Yorkie who replaced Mr. Famous after his untimely death] lay down right in the dining room as if he knew this would be his home. It was a house for living, and it remained one."

In a further attempt to cement their failing marriage, she and Ferrer bought a summer residence near Marbella, on Spain's Costa del Sol. "It was one of the only reckless financial decisions we ever made," she recalled. "But I guess we felt if we bought enough things together, we could create roots where there weren't any."

Newscaster Hugh Downs remembered inviting Audrey to his nearby villa. His housekeeper/cook was serving a delectable lunch of local fish and rice. "By the time all the guests were served, there was about two teaspoons of the concoction left for me," Downs recalled. "All the guests immediately began heaping on portions from their plates. My dish was passed from hand to hand. Naturally, by the time the plate was returned to me, it had more food than anyone else's. Audrey had the perfect rejoinder: 'You did plan that deliberately, didn't you?' she said. We all laughed so much. The few times my wife and I saw her again during that stay, all we did was laugh."

But in reality, things were glum at home. It was time now to pay for the new houses. William Wyler called just in time with a slick new comedy-thriller, *How to Steal a Million* that Audrey thought read a lot like *Charade*. Ever since *Roman Holiday*, she'd felt a loyalty to Wyler. He could easily persuade her to do any film, but she was glad this one was a frothier concoction than *The Children's Hour*, their last joint venture.

A madcap story of art forgery and familial loyalty, *How to Steal a Million* costarred Peter O'Toole as a detective who specializes in art-related crimes (and who is mistaken for a thief by Audrey's character). Hugh Griffith played Audrey's father, the master forger.

"I didn't want to work with her at all," O'Toole recalled. "No way. I thought she was going to be a stuck-up, prissy mannequin who would do anything to keep her hands clean. She surprised me totally.

"Audrey Hepburn knew how to get down and dirty and have some prankish good fun.

For the sequence in which we both try to steal back from a museum one of her father's creations, we were hiding in a closet. A lot of the scene took place right in those close quarters, and we really got to know each other well. We were on the same wavelength. She told me I broke her up, and indeed, a lot of takes were ruined because one or the other of us would burst into a fit of laughter. Willy would get hopping mad, but at me, not his darling Audrey. She was the one — and I think only — actor who could soften his resolve. She just had this wonderfully sweet way about her, and he was very smitten. He sent her fresh flowers for her dressing room, all white ones, I recall."

Wyler, as well as O'Toole, sensed the end of Audrey's marriage just by the fact that Ferrer wasn't around. "I had heard he ruled her on various sets," O'Toole said, "and I didn't see him once on this one. She never spoke about it, but there was this sadness that surrounded her like a shroud. She kept trying to blow it off with giggles, but as soon as she stopped laughing, I could sense her heart was about to break.

"I fell in love with Audrey Hepburn on that movie. I just wanted to mend her broken heart. But I didn't say a word, which is very unlike me. She made it very clear that she was holding up just by a thread and that any mention of the real reason for her unhappiness might send her over the edge. Don't get me wrong: There was nothing spoken. If anybody took it to a court of law, I would have to say she was very happy, on the surface, anyway. We laughed a lot. But underneath, she was desolate. You just know something like that."

She and Ferrer were still not ready to give up. Back at La Paisible, they tried to make one last go of it. They enjoyed rough-housing with Sean and his young friends, children of the farmers who surrounded them. On warm nights, they all went outside to catch fireflies. When autumn arrived, they rolled in massive piles of leaves. As winter approached, they collected wood for the fireplace. Everything was fine when all three were together, but when Audrey and Ferrer were alone, they didn't have much to say. In spite of the obvious distance which had grown between them, Audrey became pregnant in the winter of 1966. It was just before Christmas and she felt a sister or brother for Sean would be a gift for the whole family. She had hope, she said, that another baby would help forge a stronger bond with her husband.

At the Christmas pageant in Sean's school, she and Ferrer were delighted with his strong and clear delivery of a Nativity poem, and their pride in him made them both hope that his enthusiasm and verve might rub off on them. Instead, in what was becoming a familiar though no less painful occurrence, Audrey suffered another miscarriage in the week after Christmas.

"It hurt just as much as the first. It hurt just as much as the second. I'm not sure you can ever get over something like that. I kept wondering what I did wrong. Did I overdo the gardening? Was I too active? Was the stress from my career eating me up? I had no answers. But I think around that time Mel and I both knew that we weren't going to survive another disappointment like that. When Kurt called with a movie, I barely read the script, I was so eager to get out of the house."

Ironically, *Two for the Road*, directed by Stanley Donen, one of Audrey's favorite directors, turned out to be an evocative portrait of the demise of a marriage after twelve years, the same amount of time she and Ferrer had spent together. In truth, it would hurry along the end of her own somber union by opening her eyes again to the spirit of fun.

Frederic Raphael's script for *Two for the Road* — about the courtship and marriage of Joanna (Audrey) and Mark Wallace (Albert Finney) — used a highly successful flashback technique which made the standard story of a marriage gone bad seem fresh and provocative. It also required more rehearsal time than usual for the two stars, since they had to interact seamlessly in the past and the present, and make distinctions between the two with the slightest gestures.

Writers are notorious for disliking the portrayals of the characters they create. How can human flesh approximate the god- and goddesslike characteristics of an artistic creation? But Audrey's portrayal of the long-suffering — but certainly not silent — wife in *Two for the Road* caused Frederic Raphael to rave about her. "I am somewhat biased," he said, "but I don't think I have ever seen a performance more manifestly worthy of the Oscar, if that matters, than Audrey's in *Two for the Road*."

"Of course, we don't touch as much as the marriage is failing," Audrey said. "You will notice that on a second or third viewing. There are all sorts of clues as to what stage of the relationship we're in."

There were also clues that the intimacy she shared with Finney on-screen had seeped into their leisure hours as well.

Finney was more forthcoming than Audrey about the nature of their friendship: "Audrey and I met in an atmosphere conducive to romance, and from the moment we met, we got on famously. Doing a scene with her, my mind knew I was acting, but my heart didn't, and my body certainly didn't!" he told journalist Charles Higham. "Performing with Audrey was quite disturbing, actually. Playing a love scene with a woman as sexy as Audrey, you sometimes get to the edge where make-believe and reality are blurred. All that staring into each other's eyes."

According to Donen, who had directed Audrey in both *Funny Face* and *Charade*, she was a changed woman on *Two for the Road*. "The Audrey I saw during the making of this film I didn't even know. She overwhelmed me. She was so free, so happy. I never saw her like that. So young!"

Two for the Road was Audrey's metamorphosis. She was shedding the skin of domination both of her husband and her look, and the liberation made her giddy. Gone was the severely simple Givenchy style from which she had rarely deviated; in its place was a softer hairstyle, freer clothing, and dresses right off the rack for the first time in her life.

After a day of filming in Paris, she and Finney would avoid the hot spots in favor of an obscure bistro off the beaten track. They would order heaping plates of food (which Audrey barely touched) and bottles of cheap wine and just laugh and tell jokes until the waiters started to pack up.

What happened next on those evenings doesn't really matter. Audrey had broken her bond with Ferrer, whether or not she had broken her vows.

At the cast party on the final day of shooting, every male member of the crew (there were actually two crews, one English and one French) wanted to dance with her. "She danced until she had blisters on her feet," said costar William Daniels. "She must have been exhausted — but she made sure they all got their dance."

"It was no secret that Audrey's marriage with Mel was not a happy one," said Henry Rogers, her former publicist. "It seemed to me that she loved him more than he loved her, and it was frustrating for her not to have her love returned in kind. She had confided these feelings to me and a number of other intimate friends many times. She never complained, but I always saw the sadness in her eyes."

Ironically, she would have to erase all emotions from her eyes for her next role, which — marriage on the rocks or not — would be produced by her husband. In *Wait Until Dark*, Audrey would play a blind woman terrorized by three thugs.

In Lausanne, she studied with Wilhelm Streiff, a physician who specialized in treating the blind at a clinic he had founded several years earlier.

"I threw myself into the task," Audrey said. "There were all sorts of rumors flying about Mel and Marisol [the shapely Spanish performer with whom he was working on several projects], and I was extremely hurt by them. *Wait Until Dark* provided me with a real outlet; it was quite a task, learning to walk without seeing, and I don't think if my home life were more tranquil I would have thrown myself into learning to move as the blind move with quite so much fervor. It took my mind off the sadness at home, and it helped me feel good about myself. I guess I also wanted to prove to Mel that I was a fine actress still, that I could do it, that I could make him proud."

Ferrer helped negotiate Audrey a $1 million salary for *Wait Until Dark*, an astounding sum for a movie that was not an epic or a musical. They agreed to try to put their marital difficulties aside during the filming; both Audrey and Ferrer rightly felt that their problems could adversely affect the other cast members and ruin the movie.

"I gave a tea for the press," Audrey recalled with distaste. "We had loads of reporters and photographers over to the house we'd rented in Beverly Hills and made it perfectly clear we were perfectly happy. It was a very trying time."

In fact, Audrey was so ambivalent about working with Ferrer that she tried to persuade Warner Brothers to allow her to film the movie in Europe, where at least she could be close to her beloved son. A harshly worded telegram from Jack Warner made it clear the entire movie would be filmed in the United States, "where it [the story] took place."

Based on the highly successful 1966 Broadway play directed by Arthur Penn and starring Lee Remick, *Wait Until Dark* was a thriller, like *Sorry, Wrong Number* and *Gaslight*, that derived its scariest moments by exaggerating the vulnerability of a woman alone and playing on what could happen to her.

The plot of the movie is irresistible: Susie Hendrix (Audrey), recently blind, is left alone in her basement apartment in Manhattan when her husband (Efrem Zimbalist, Jr.) is lured away by a hoax. The three perpetrators of the ruse (Alan Arkin, Richard Crenna, and Jack Weston) then show up to search for a heroin-filled antique musical doll unwittingly in her possession.

Director Terence Young, best known as the overseer of several James Bond movies, would give the movie a heart-stopping pace that caused audiences around the country to scream aloud at its most frightening moments. But in the beginning, he, too, was most concerned with Audrey's giving a realistic performance, and in New York, he introduced her to several pupils from the Lighthouse for the Blind. They taught her to distinguish various sounds and helped ease her fear of the darkness. "The best thing I learned was how to put lipstick on without a mirror," Audrey said. "I count it as one of my major accomplishments."

"We would walk around together with blindfolds," Young recalled, "but Audrey's patience won her the ability to learn to do things without sight, while I would get too frustrated. She was fascinated by the whole process, you could just tell. She'd talk to me about the feel of things and what they sound like with such highly descriptive language that I sensed she was discovering a new way of seeing, herself."

Her heightened appreciation of all of her senses led Audrey to insist upon afternoon tea every day during filming. Unbelievably, the production would shut down every afternoon precisely at 4:00 P.M. and the cast and crew would sip tea, eat dainty sandwiches, and talk quietly with one another.

"Looking back," said Richard Crenna, "it's

still hard to believe we really did have tea — in china cups, I might add — every day we worked. It was an amazingly civilized thing to do, and only Audrey would have thought of it. But it brought us into a close camaraderie without the sloppy familiarity that would have resulted from our drinking together every evening. This was tea — and it was polite, genteel, and oh so Audrey."

The strain of working with Ferrer was beginning to take its toll, however. As she did in so many times of stress, she just stopped eating. Jack Warner, who had worried about her health throughout the making of *My Fair Lady*, now wondered if she was going to make it through *Wait Until Dark*. After seeing her gaunt face and progressively scrawnier body on some of the dailies, he sent her baskets of fruit and boxes of chocolates. Although she thanked him profusely, the gifts went uneaten.

To make matters worse, Ferrer was trying to interest studios in another production of the tragic love story *Mayerling*, but this time around he wanted Catherine Deneuve to play the role Audrey had done so well.

"I was in a bad way," she recalled. "I missed Sean tremendously and I worried night and day what would happen if Mel and I didn't make it. My own childhood was ruined when my father left. It was as if I didn't have a childhood after that. I had to grow up and be a good girl and help my mother, and I never could scream and say I wanted my daddy. I was so afraid for Sean that I vowed to stay with Mel."

In fact, even after there was no hope of a lasting reconciliation, Audrey became pregnant again in July of 1967. She lost the baby in August, "and I knew the ruse was over," she said. In September, just before *Wait Until Dark* was officially released, lawyers announced the end of the Ferrer-Hepburn marriage in a succinct statement that belied the pain and suffering each of them had endured:

"Audrey Hepburn, thirty-eight, and Mel Ferrer, fifty, have separated after thirteen years of marriage. Ferrer is in Paris and Miss Hepburn is at their home in Switzerland with their son, Sean, seven."

Audrey would never say anything to diminish her ex-husband in the eyes of their son. She sadly explained to him that Mommy and Daddy would not be living together any longer, but that they both loved him as much as ever.

"It brought me back to the time when my own parents separated," Audrey recalled. "And as much as I wanted to believe those same words that were said to me, I couldn't help then but think it was all my fault.

"But then it came to me: If I thought some-where in my soul that my own parents' divorce was because of me, then I was perpetuating all this unhappiness. I was giving a legacy of sadness to my son. I did my best to get rid of the guilt I had — misplaced though it was, it was real — over my own parents' breakup, so that I could make crystal clear to Sean he had nothing to do with the troubles between his mommy and daddy.

"I never wanted to be divorced," Audrey continued. "To this day, I hate the word. I cringe when it's applied to me. My own ideal was always to be married once, and forever. It's the way I was. I thought a marriage be-tween two good people should last until one of them died, and then I believed the other person would just live quietly on the mem-ories.

"But life didn't work out that way. Mel and I were both good people, but we didn't forge a lasting bond. Life, and celebrity, got in the way."

Audrey would begin to blame celebrity — and the rigors of living up to an image that was not real — for a lot of her heartache. She made up her mind to carve a new life for herself, one that did not rely on bright lights.

Chapter 24

She couldn't eat. The more she tried to force something down — a piece of toast, an orange — the more the food disgusted her. She was even having a hard time making meals for Sean, because the aromas from cooking sickened her.

A month after her marriage to Ferrer broke up, Audrey's weight had dropped to an alarming ninety-four pounds. "I had never seen her so thin," said Germaine Lefebvre, the French-born actress better known as Capucine and one of Audrey's closest friends. "Her cheekbones were so pointy, I was afraid if I kissed her they would hurt. And she wouldn't leave the house. I felt she was on the verge of a nervous breakdown, and I would ask her what good she would be for Sean if she had to be hospitalized."

Capucine thought that if Audrey were paid a little male attention, she might rally. Rumors of Ferrer's indiscriminate dating devastated Audrey. Capucine persuaded her to go to the house in Marbella for a change of scenery, and once there, she started to go out in the evenings, often on the arm of Prince Alfonso de Bourbon-Dampierre or the Spanish bull-fighter Antonio Ordonez.

Gossip columnists reported her soulful gazes at Prince Alfonso. In the middle of crowded Marbella nightclubs, she seemed completely engrossed in what he was saying, not hearing anyone else. It looked to all the world like love.

"It was a complete act," Audrey said. "I have never been so scared in all my life. I felt completely alone, and my friends had convinced me it didn't have to be that way. But I didn't want to start dating. Once you reach a certain age, the idea of telling a stranger your whole life story — in other words, of getting to know someone and letting them get to know you — is a frightening prospect. During those first tentative steps I took to socialize, I hated every minute. I thought maybe if I looked interested enough I could avoid the whole courtship thing and just quickly get married again. I wanted desperately to be married. At least then I wouldn't have to say I was divorced!"

Friends around the world became worried about Audrey, and the sense of desperation they saw in her. Lollo and Lorean Gaetani Lovatelli, part of the "fun" aristocracy she occasionally joined at parties in various European capitals, invited her to dinner at their stately palace on Rome's Piazza Lovatelli. It was an extremely low-key affair, with all the guests lamenting the boring months ahead with nothing to look forward to except a costume ball in Venice during Mardi Gras. Despite her pedigree as the daughter of a baroness, Audrey felt out of place among the jaded jet-setters. But she soon realized they made it their business to pamper anyone in their set who might be feeling low; they took care of their own. Despite the fact that she found the conversations vapid and wearying, she also felt comforted in their midst. Tedium aside, at least she would not be alone.

Princess Olympia Torlonia had just that in mind when she invited Audrey for a cruise of the Greek islands with her and her fabulously wealthy husband, French gasoline king Paul Annik Weiller. The two-week cruise in June of 1968 would be just what the doctor ordered, Princess Olympia said. It would be relaxing and revitalizing. There would be several other guests, she said. They were all congenial.

Audrey had eyes for only one of them: Andrea Mario Dotti, M.D., a wealthy young psychiatrist who specialized in treating women and depression. He was solicitous and charming, empathetic and warm, everything Mel could never be.

Sunning together on the prow of the boat, they spent hours talking alone. Dotti was captivated by the innocence of the world-renowned movie star. It was clear to all aboard that he was quickly falling in love with her.

She was more reticent. Audrey was not at all averse to a little shipboard romance, but as much as she purported to want to get married again, she didn't think Dotti was a suitable candidate. He was young — nine years younger than she and, more telling, twenty-one years younger than Ferrer. But he was extremely persuasive in his wooing, and his gentleness delighted Audrey.

Born in Naples on March 18, 1938, Dotti also descended from a long line of counts and countesses, but unlike Audrey, his regal lineage was well endowed. Audrey was the first to admit to herself that she liked the idea that Dotti was financially comfortable, but she liked even more that he worked long and hard at his psychiatric clinic for a token salary. His dedication to his profession proved to her that he had character. But these were mere musings to herself. She was afraid to speak of her growing attachment to the handsome young doctor to any of her friends, and especially her always-protective mother.

The trip turned out to be one of the first real vacations she'd had in years. Ferrer was always too ambitious and too often frustrated to relax for long. Schemes to produce movies, or to popularize himself or Audrey, continually interfered with any fun. But with Dotti, and the rest of her European entourage, the talk was always of the beauty of the tiny, round-domed houses against the blue of the water in Crete, of the possibility that Santorini was really the lost island of Atlantis, of the bracing taste of retsina with a wedge of feta and a fresh tomato. They lived each day in the present, and in the present, Audrey and Dotti began to express their love for one another.

Then Dotti made a startling revelation, one that would endear him to Audrey for the rest of her life. " 'I've met you before, you know,' he told me. 'And you don't remember, do you? That saddens me so. You were filming *Roman Holiday*, and I came out to see you. I was barely a teenager,' he said, 'but I fell in love with you then. You were the first woman for whom I remember having sexual urges. I fantasized about you for the rest of my youth. You took my hand when we met and squeezed it gently — more familiar than a shake — and I never forgot you.' "

Audrey, however, had no recollection of the

meeting. "That's because he was such a young boy!" she said. "When Andrea told me that, it was clear to me our age difference would again foul us up if we stayed together. I tried to rationalize it — we loved one another, we had similar interests. He was older than me intellectually; that was true. But always, in the back of my mind, I remembered that Andrea was once a boy when I was a woman."

At thirty-nine, she felt just as young as his thirty. But she knew, too, that someday she would turn into a mature woman while he remained a young man. Still, she decided not to think about that.

What really forged a bond between them was the fact that both their sets of parents had divorced when they were young and neither of them had seen their father much after the breakup. They each suffered from a profound fear of abandonment because of this, although they approached their fears in very different ways. Dotti had trouble with commitment, preferring to surround himself with hordes of adoring women rather than count on (and possibly be disappointed by) one love interest. Audrey, on the other hand, flung herself headlong into monogamous relationships, not actually knowing what she should look for in a mate because she didn't have a father figure with whom to compare him.

Dotti did have a stepfather however, Vero Roberti, the distinguished correspondent for the daily newspaper *Corriere della Sera*, with whom he shared confidences. Roberti and Dotti's mother, Paola, were initially distraught when their beloved son mentioned his growing involvement with Audrey. An actress for a wife? Heaven forbid. A divorced woman with a child? An older woman?

She easily won them over, however, during her first visit to their home over the 1968 Christmas holidays. After midnight mass, when the family exchanged gifts, Paola took Audrey aside and told her she was the nicest present her son could have ever given her.

"The family embraced me as if I had always been part of it," Audrey recalled. "They were an extremely aristocratic clan, educated, wise, but they were also some of the most loving people I have ever met. If I had any doubts about the marriage before I met them, they were completely gone after that Christmas together. I loved the idea of expanding my family in one easy step."

Marriage would bring Audrey an expanded immediate family, which she loved. Dotti had three brothers — an electrical engineer, a banker, and a sociologist — and when they all got together with their wives and children and Dotti and Audrey and Sean, she was never more content.

After announcing their banns in the post office of Tolochenaz, Audrey and Dotti were quietly married on January 18, 1969, in the town hall of nearby Morges. The local registrar, Denise Rattaz, had to momentarily stop the ceremony because she was crying. "I had never seen a more beautiful bride before that day, and I never would," she said.

Audrey was dressed in a simple, short, pink Givenchy ensemble with sleeves that petaled out like tulips at the wrist. "She was so serene that day," recalled Capucine, who witnessed the ceremony along with Yul Brynner's wife Doris. "I believe she had never been happier." According to Paul Weiller, who introduced the couple on that fateful cruise of the Greek isles, "There was no doubt in my mind that this marriage was a great thing for both of them. It gave Andrea someone to love and it gave Audrey security."

The idyll would not last long, however. Dotti had trouble loving just one woman and that made Audrey terribly insecure.

But throughout the winter and spring of 1969, Audrey reveled in her new life. She and Dotti had located a marvelous apartment overlooking the Tiber River near the Ponte Vittorio in Rome, and Audrey delighted in decorating it, often accepting wonderful antiques lent to her by her doting mother-in-law. Sean adjusted beautifully to life with a stepfather, and he seemed to delight in living in a city, exploring every inch of Rome.

Audrey often walked her husband to work in the morning, returned home to see Sean off to school, spent the morning planning the evening's meal with the cook, then did the marketing herself.

"I was in heaven, pure and simple," she said. "I had wanted so long to actually run a household day in and day out. With Mel, we were never in one place for more than a month or two at a time, so even at home, things felt temporary. In Italy, I could finally develop a routine. I think I probably overdid the 'wife and mother' thing a little in those first couple of months, but then I calmed down and was never happier. I began to shop for clothing and really enjoy it. All those years of people raving about my style, and for that brief moment, I knew what they meant."

Audrey's simple elegance was at its height. Not only did she purchase more of her beloved Givenchys, she also began buying Valentino, another classic couturier. She finally began to like how she looked, just a little bit.

The family went to little trattorias for long lunches, or spent leisurely, stolen afternoons at the Gambrino Beach Club. Countess Gaetani, who had introduced Audrey to her hosts for the Greek cruise, invited the Dottis for weekend sojourns to her spectacular property on the Islo Giglio in the Mediterranean. They toured museums together. They even went to the movies like ordinary people.

Audrey loved being a homebody in Italy, and the sweet regularity of her days made her happier than she'd ever been. The honeymoon — for that's what daily living felt like to her — was lasting longer than she'd ever hoped. When she became pregnant in April, she thought she had finally found the world of domestic bliss she had always sought.

"I was beginning to think I'd finally found peace," Audrey recalled. "In my usual dramatic way, I decided I never wanted to work again in motion pictures; I would just tend to my family. It was giving me so much satisfaction to be a wife and mother, I wished for a time I had never become an actress."

Her pregnancy proved difficult, however, and the doctors advised complete bed rest to avoid a miscarriage. She decided to return to Tolochenaz for this period, so she could at least be awakened by the sounds of birds every morning. She would have less trouble with confinement in the country than in the city. Besides, Dotti was working extremely long hours on a project at his clinic and Sean was thriving at the Lycée Français in Rome.

But the last six months of her pregnancy were extremely uncomfortable for Audrey and the rumors about her husband's philandering made matters worse. What Audrey never imagined is that Dotti would continue his wild social life after their marriage. Not only did it continue, it seemed to accelerate.

Night after night after he finished up at his clinic, Dotti was photographed on the arm of a beautiful young woman at some of the hottest night spots in Rome. In some photos, he was seen biting their ears. In others, he and his date were kissing passionately. One woman with whom he was photographed more than once, the model Daniela, was a notorious party girl. The official story was that Dotti was offering psychiatric help to her for drug addiction. The trouble was, Daniela publicly stated that she didn't have a drug problem.

Audrey was distraught. "I tried to reason with myself that my husband was Roman, this was not unusual, it was the way he was brought up. But none of that worked for me. I felt extremely rejected, especially since I was about to have his baby. I thought seriously about leaving him, but I thought the decision would have lasting effects on Sean. He seemed to get along with his stepfather, and I didn't want to disrupt his life again." Once again, Audrey was making excuses for the man in her life, who was making her miserable.

Still, on weekends, when Dotti flew to Switzerland to visit his bedridden wife, they entertained one another with stories of their childhoods and little games they invented on the spot. "We did not talk about infidelity," Audrey said. "That would have been much too painful for me. I was of the school then, 'Out of sight, out of mind.' I didn't see any mistresses around, so I chose not to believe in them. What I mean is, I ignored them. I was having a baby, for God's sake, and I couldn't handle the end of the fairy tale before it had even begun."

On February 8, 1970, at the Cantonial Hospital in Lausanne, Audrey, forty, gave birth by cesarean section to a seven-pound, eight-ounce boy. Both she and her husband were ecstatic, as were the rest of the Dottis in Rome.

"We decided to call him Luca, a name that has been in Andrea's family for years," Audrey explained. "I was so thrilled at finally being able to have another child, I was completely optimistic that things between Andrea and I would work out. I mean, we had so much going for us."

Like the dutiful wife that she always wanted to be, Audrey took a decided interest in her husband's work and his patients, often stopping by at the clinic for afternoon tea.

She made all the travel arrangements for him when he flew around the world to medical conventions, often accompanying him on the trips. She organized lunches with the wives of Dotti's fellow doctors, at which they mostly discussed their children. It was a fairly staid, fairly uneventful life, and Audrey loved every minute of it.

A few projects were offered in the early seventies, but she immediately turned them down, telling producers she had a brand-new career as a full-time wife and mother. She passed on *Nicholas and Alexandra* (Janet Suzman eventually played the part of the Russian czarina); a role opposite Richard Burton in *Jackpot*; a movie by *Wait Until Dark* director Terence Young; and a part opposite Elizabeth Taylor in *Father's Day*, a movie about two divorcees who set up house together. Without her involvement, the latter two movies were never made.

The writer Garson Kanin was desperate to get Audrey for *A Thousand Summers*, the proposed movie from his bestselling novel about a lifelong affair between a pharmacist and a diplomat's wife. "I didn't think any other actress could do the part. Audrey had the right mixture of mischievousness and sophistication. George C. Scott wanted to play opposite her. I wanted Dustin Hoffman or Jack Lemmon. When I mentioned Audrey's name to both of them, they were immediately interested." Audrey turned down the project. The movie was never made.

But her friends advised her she was being foolish in not working at all. David Niven, a lifelong friend and fellow resident of Switzerland, advised her to go back to work, if only to show Dotti that she could still charm the world, albeit perhaps not her own husband. "David never, never approved of the men I married," Audrey said. "He thought Mel used me, and he thought Andrea ignored me. He treated me like a little sister a lot of the time, but I know he had my best interests at heart. He told me in no uncertain terms if I wanted my husband to stop straying, I should go back to work."

The movie she chose was *Robin and Marian*, Richard Lester's delightful story of a middle-aged Robin Hood (Sean Connery) who, after fighting the Crusades and wandering the Holy Land for twenty years, returns to Sherwood Forest accompanied by his old pal Little John (Nicol Williamson) and lays claim to his long-lost love Maid Marian (Audrey), by now the abbess of a priory.

The rekindling of their romance is beautifully rendered. "My confessions were the envy of the convent," she tells her old boyfriend. "But you never wrote."

"I didn't know how," he says simply. And in that moment, he redeems himself in her eyes.

Audrey loved the fact that the movie promoted an enduring romance, and one that was shown as lusty even in middle age. If she wanted to prove something to Dotti, it was that she was still desirable just as she was, looking her age at forty-six, not hiding from it.

But she never expected to look quite so much her age. Filming outside of Pamplona in the summer of 1975 proved more arduous than any of her previous shoots, including *The Nun's Story*. Spain was enduring record heat waves that, added to Audrey's severe case of dysentery, turned her into a dehydrated bag of nerves.

"We arranged the shooting to accommodate her younger son's school holidays," said director Richard Lester, "which was very important to her, because she was concerned that she spend as much time with him as possible.

"She had been accustomed to being dressed by Givenchy, and she had just one costume in this picture, made out of a thick burlap material, so it must have been a terrible shock to her to think, after eight years away from the screen, 'Is this what the world of film has come to?' Yet she took it with immense good grace."

"I had been away from movies for a long, long time," she recalled, "and I was plenty nervous. Lester was always in a big hurry. I never remember doing more than two takes on anything. He didn't pussyfoot around, nor did he coddle his stars. I missed the strokes, but I kept going without them."

And it paid off. "The moment she appears on the screen is startling," wrote *Time* magazine, "not for her thorough, gentle command, not even for her beauty, which seems heightened, renewed. It is rather that we are reminded how long it has been since an actress has so beguiled us and captured our imagination. Hepburn is unique and, now, almost alone."

Chapter 25

David Niven was right: At least for a little while, Audrey's return to the glamour of the screen inspired jealousy in Dotti and rekindled the flame of her marriage.

Dotti detested the idea she'd become a full-time actress again, so her foray back in *Robin and Marian* was enough to keep him on his toes. Like Ferrer, he was slightly resentful of his wife's celebrity. But at least Dotti was never in competition with her. He just wanted to make sure she'd be at home when he needed her. Whenever that was.

In a nutshell, Audrey felt manipulated. When Dotti wanted a wife — for a social function, say, or when someone in the family celebrated a christening or a wedding — Audrey was expected to be dutifully by his side. But when he decided to carouse on the town without her (and she never wanted to go clubbing), Audrey was expected to make herself scarce.

Since the boys were both thriving and busy with school, she decided to spend more time considering the many scripts she was still being sent.

One day during the summer of 1976 in the living room of the penthouse apartment near Ponte Vittorio, she answered the phone expecting to hear from her agent, Kurt Frings.

Instead her worst fears were confirmed. Kidnappers were on the line, threatening both Sean and Luca. Italy's Red Brigades were at the height of their terror campaign, and Audrey had often obsessed about the possibility of kidnapping. This single call was all she needed to forge ahead with her own plan: Sean and Luca were spirited away to Leonardo da Vinci Airport that afternoon, and by nightfall they were safely ensconced at La Paisible.

"I was determined to protect my children from harm," Audrey said. "There was no question about that. I guess that scare gave me strength, or at least reminded me that I was still strong, no matter how depressed I was over my marriage or my career. You sometimes need to be tested in order to show your true grit. Before that voice on the phone threatened the people I held most dear, I didn't know I had it in me to make a decision about anything. After that, it was easy. I had the energy to defend my boys."

Audrey enrolled them in Le Rosey, an exclusive Swiss boarding school that catered to the children of industrialists and film stars, and they made an immediate and healthy adjustment.

Her husband, however, was not so lucky. While she was with the boys in Switzerland, Dotti was nearly abducted in broad daylight outside of his clinic in Rome. Four gun-toting kidnappers attempted to shove Dotti into their blue Mercedes getaway car. He resisted. They knocked him down to the pavement with the butt of their guns. He began bleeding profusely, but he screamed so loudly that two policemen began to chase the kidnappers. They got away, but without Dotti.

"I was paralyzed by the kidnapping attempt," Audrey said. "I lived with irrational fears anyway, so when something real happened to someone close to me, I fell apart. If our marriage had a slight chance before that incident, it was doomed afterward. I was too afraid to come to Rome much. Andrea was too brave, too resilient to be cowed by terrorism, but that scared me, too. I wanted a husband to share the daily things with. But he felt he had to stay in Rome no matter what, and I couldn't go there no matter what."

She did, however, travel to America to help promote *Robin and Marian*, and was treated as if she were a true princess from Rome on holiday in New York and Los Angeles.

"It was too much, too exaggerated," she said about her overwhelming reception. "I felt as if I had died and returned to life. I guess very few actresses had retired and come back." Audrey was wrong; many actresses had. But they were not the stars of *Roman Holiday*, or *Breakfast at Tiffany's*, or *My Fair Lady*. In Hollywood, Jack Valenti, president of the Motion Picture Association of America, spoke for all of her fans when he addressed her from the stage of the Santa Monica Civic Center. "Welcome back, Audrey," he said. "You've been away too long."

She was beginning to feel the same way. Her marriage to Dotti was continuing to disintegrate. His philandering continued, but now that she was living primarily in Switzerland, she realized it didn't bother her as much. It was a matter of "out of sight, out of mind." She was forced by circumstances to live without him, and she was living. That was the first incontrovertible evidence that her marriage was over. She was surviving on her own. Once Audrey stopped caring, there was no point in continuing.

Publicly, however, she kept up a good front. "My marriage is basically happy," she told one reporter who did not stick to her rules and ask questions only about *Robin and Marian*. "We have our differences, our disagreements, but we cope. We do our best at coping."

But Audrey was not doing her best at coping. As much as she realized her marriage was over, she could not bring herself to confront Dotti and officially end it. "My pride was involved, of course," she said, "and also my overwhelming fear of being left alone. Even when I was doing the leaving, I was afraid I would be left. It's irrational, yes, but also very real."

She wanted to get out of the marriage, but she also wanted to make sure she would have a project to occupy her and take her mind off her loneliness. Consequently, she made one of the worst film choices of her whole career. Terence Young, the director of *Wait Until Dark*, persuaded Audrey to do Sidney Sheldon's *Bloodline*, a lurid melodrama about sex, violence, and greed, a stark departure from her usual fare.

She may also have been more interested in the tax advantages of *Bloodline*, which was being filmed under the auspices of a West German tax shelter, than she was in its titillating soap opera plot about a woman thrust into the world of business.

She insisted on, however, and won, many concessions. The majority of her scenes were shot in Rome. There was only a minor stay in New York. If she had had to fly to Copenhagen, Sardinia, and Munich with the rest of the cast, she would have turned down the leading role of Elizabeth Rolfe. It would have interfered too much with Luca's school schedule. In addition, because she was a mother first now, scenes of gratuitous sex and violence were excised from the script. Sidney Sheldon agreed to tamper with his prose just to keep Audrey. He became so enamored of her that he diluted some of his best sex scenes so as not to offend her.

"She had a quality no other actress had: a curious combination of lady and pixie," said Sheldon. "She was a joy to work with — enormous talent and no ego."

"It was an awful time for me," Audrey recalled. "I began worrying about money for me and the boys when I thought about leaving Andrea, and I suppose the million dollars for *Bloodline* was a big inducement to taking on the picture. It offered financial security, which meant more to me than artistic value at the time. And I felt I had to have something to do or I would go crazy."

While filming, she became friendly with costar Ben Gazzara. He was going through a difficult time in his marriage to Janice Rule, and they commiserated often about wedded woes. "He was a lifesaver without even knowing it," Audrey said. "Just to hear someone else going through the confusion and bitterness of a breakup made me feel less alone. We had these rambling philosophical discussions about the meaning of love and commitment and really became good friends. *Bloodline* may have been awful, but it was redeemed in my eyes because I met Ben on it."

During the filming, the cast had a midnight spaghetti party. Liza Minnelli came and gave an extremely gushing toast to Audrey. In response, Audrey got on the table and started dancing, leaping with joy. "It came out of her sweetness," recalled Gazzara, "out of her being embarrassed by the praise. I thought it was charming, better than words. Speaking words would have made her cry. So she danced. How she danced around the spaghetti plates, I don't know. But she didn't break one of them."

When the movie opened, it received the worst reviews of any film in Audrey's career. "It is a ghastly film," wrote George Bishop in London's *Sunday Express*, "hackneyed, humorless, grubby, and so disjointed as to be a pain to follow." But the critics were still kind to Audrey. The only thing worth seeing in *Bloodline*, they agreed, was Audrey Hepburn as the dutiful daughter who inherits her father's enormous pharmaceutical empire and must do battle with her rivals within and without her family. Most said she rose above the material and instilled a surprising vulnerability into a stock character.

Audrey needed to hear that she still had the ability to charm audiences. She was getting worried that she had irreparably sabotaged her career by ignoring it for so long and by picking so dreadful a commercial vehicle as *Bloodline*. Gazzara told her a bold move was in order. If she did not wish to be perceived as a has-been, he advised, she had to avoid big commercial movies for the next few years. Hollywood had changed, he said. The important movies were not being made by studios any longer. The independent feature films now had all the cachet. He persuaded her to take a look at Peter Bogdanovich's *They All Laughed*, the movie he had just agreed to do.

A light farce in which two detectives, played by Gazzara and John Ritter, fall in love with the "unfaithful" women they are tailing (Audrey and Dorothy Stratten), *They All Laughed* is a romantic comedy of the old school, with plenty of surface charm and a melancholy knowingness about the futility of true love. Yet its plot is quite contemporary and was eerily similar to Audrey's own life.

In the movie, she plays an extremely wealthy, extremely attractive tycoon's wife who has not known love for a long time. In fact, it is her husband's guilt over his own infidelities that convinces him to hire the private eye and unwittingly encourage the affair between her and the detective. Their relationship in the movie is comfortable and bittersweet. "This is where I turn into a pumpkin," she tells her lover after one tryst.

Yet in real life, Audrey enjoyed no such self-knowledge. She became completely enamored of Gazzara, looking at him long and longingly throughout the shoot, ignoring the fact that she'd landed her son Sean a small part in the film and he was around to witness his mother's lovesickness.

"It was a very odd time," Audrey said. "I didn't know what I wanted, but I knew I had to want something or else I would be better off dead. I was having a hard time getting enthusiastic about anything. I could go through the motions, you might not notice it if you just spent a little time with me, but inside I was feeling pretty empty."

A month after *They All Laughed* completed filming, a player in the movie and Bogdanovich's most recent girlfriend, former *Playboy* centerfold Dorothy Stratten, was brutally murdered by her estranged husband, Paul Snider. (Her death became the subject of Bob Fosse's movie *Star 80*.) Audrey was distraught over Stratten's death, a fact that was complicated by rumors that Audrey herself was having an affair with Bogdanovich.

The director became inconsolable over the tragedy of losing Stratten. He made a hasty decision to distribute *They All Laughed* himself, to prevent anyone from using Stratten's death to enhance the promotion of the movie.

His decision hurt the chances for *They All Laughed*. Although the movie was acclaimed when it debuted at the Venice Film Festival in the summer of 1981 and *Variety* called it "probably Bogdanovich's best film to date," its release in the United States was delayed by Bogdanovich's inexperience in distribution. When it finally opened in New York that winter, the critical response was lukewarm, and the movie languished at the box office. Audrey had expected it to redeem her from the mistake of *Bloodline*. When it did not, she began to feel her career was over.

Her friends rallied to her side. Close chum Connie Wald, widow of producer Jerry Wald, threw a small dinner party at her Bel Air mansion and insisted Audrey join her, Billy and Audrey Wilder, and Robert Wolders, the extremely handsome young widower of legendary actress Merle Oberon. He was grief-stricken over Oberon's death several months earlier, Wald explained, and it was one of his first nights out. To insure Wolders's presence, Wald had told him that Audrey was extremely depressed and might be cheered up by spending time with someone else from the Netherlands.

"It was a time in both our lives when we were very sad," Audrey said. "We had that in common. That was enough to keep us seeing one another as friends for a long time."

On that first evening, from the moment they discovered they had spent their childhoods in nearby towns in Holland, Audrey and Wolders never stopped talking to one another. A former actor who had costarred in the television series *Laredo*, Wolders had made a successful switch to producing, mostly movies in northern Europe. "It was friendship at first sight," Audrey said. "But that was not enough to cause us to fall in love. That happened later."

In the ensuing months, on the pretext of business, Wolders often mysteriously showed up in whatever city Audrey happened to be. "I came more and more to rely on him," she said. "He made himself indispensable as a friend and confidant. If he didn't call for a few days, I began to miss him. It was a gradual falling in love, but that's what it was. I must say it took me completely by surprise. I thought that part of my life was over, that I would never have the romance I dreamed of as a girl. Then, when you least expect it . . ."

They had much in common. They were both attractive and reticent and gentle and Dutch. They both had suffered greatly during the war. However strong he looked, Wolders endured terrible headaches that were the direct result of wartime deprivation. Audrey understood his residual pain. He realized her eating disorders were the result of her childhood traumas. They empathized with one another.

"Audrey, in the beginning, liked me as a friend and was trying to find me a good woman!" Wolders said. "I always was attracted to her, I loved her quite from the start, but I knew she had given up on love and I had to go very slowly. That was fine with me."

Their courtship inched along. Although her divorce from Dotti did not officially come through until 1982, her marriage to him was long over. "Robbie was extremely persistent," Audrey remembered, "but not in an overbearing way. He would call regularly, and we had some of the best times on the telephone! It was wonderful — I didn't even have to get dressed to see him. It's funny, but in all the years I knew Merle, I had never met Robbie with her. She raved about him — how loving, how devoted — but I had a different image of him, someone not quite his own person. That was not the case at all. He is completely comfortable with himself, serene. He has definite likes and dislikes. But he genuinely wants another person in his life, as I do, and is willing to compromise and share to achieve harmony."

When he would first come to visit at Tolochenaz, Audrey introduced him to her mother and her sons as a good friend. "I often wonder if our romance would have progressed if we were both living in Los Angeles," she said. "I don't know. Had we lived nearby, everything would have been easy and comfortable. But Robbie had to come a long way to see me in Switzerland, and when he got here, there weren't parties to go to and movies to catch. We were left with each other. I'm so grateful for the peace and quiet that contributed to our falling in love."

He moved into the house at Tolochenaz in 1981, and he never left. "It took me such a long, long time," Audrey said, "but I am finally and completely happy. I have fun with Robbie, which is something I never even knew to want."

Wolders eased his way into the hearts of Audrey's children by making it clear that he had no desire to replace their fathers. He even made it clear that he would respect their wishes if they didn't want to get to know him at all. It was their choice; he would not force himself on anyone. Sean, now a strappingly handsome twenty-one-year-old, respected Wolders from the start, but eleven-year-old Luca was initially a little resentful of the new man in his mother's life. Wolders remained patient. He didn't foist a false friendship on the boy. In time, Luca came to respect him, especially after it became obvious Wolders made his mother so happy. "I used to tease Robbie that our relationship was inevitable," Audrey recalled. "I played the part of the same woman accused of being a lesbian in the remake of *The Children's Hour* that Merle played in the original [*These Three*]. With a coincidence like that, how could we go wrong?"

The Baroness was thrilled from the start. She had made clear her dislike for the controlling Ferrer and the philandering Dotti, and she delighted in the fact that Wolders was not only sensitive and loyal, he was Dutch. Any misgivings about his less aristocratic roots were completely erased by his devotion to Audrey and the people she held dear. As her mother's health began to decline due to old age and the onset of rheumatism, the Baroness began to use a wheelchair. Audrey's lifelong friend Henry Gris recalled that Wolders would often push the Baroness around the gardens of the house and speak to her in Dutch. "They really liked one another," Audrey recalled. "It was a joy to witness."

At long last, someone was as completely in love with Audrey as she was with him. At home, the two of them spent their days puttering in the garden, reading aloud to one another, and reflecting on the joys of their life together.

But they also spent more time in Los Angeles and New York. "I was of an age and station when the charity circuit beckoned loud and clear," Audrey recalled. "There were also so many tributes I was invited to. This had been going on for quite some time, but I always ignored it. With Robbie, though, I had more fun going out. We enjoyed each other's company so much that I was less nervous at big parties. For once, it was fun getting dressed up. Robbie was always so complimentary."

With the support of Wolders, Audrey finally began viewing herself as attractive. For the first time in her life, the woman who had inspired so many others to imitate her classic chic actually began to understand what all the fuss was about.

"Until Hepburn appeared, there weren't beauties who weren't voluptuous," recalled designer Isaac Mizrahi in *Interview* magazine. "People thought that to be gaminelike was not beautiful. I'm sure she never felt really beautiful. And yet there were millions of women who wanted to look like her.

"In a lot of ways, she was the beginning of minimalism . . . She had a very graphic face and body. You could take that face and turn it into a flat surface. Her body probably inspired a lot of the clothes Givenchy did for her. The clothes that she wore were not fussy. It was really very simple clothing. They all had a line or a little bit of shape or something. They were not about beading and ruffles and stuff like that. Of course, she wore feathers and froufrou and all that stuff, but it was always so simple, you didn't even notice it. You just kind of noticed her throat, her face, her eyes.

"Yet she immortalized those clothes. There's that scene in *Funny Face* where she's wearing a little hooded parka, an anorak kind of jacket, and a black turtleneck and skinny black pants and black loafers, and it's like the only perfect American look."

Once, at the Kennedy Center tribute to Cary Grant, Rex Harrison, introducing Audrey, said in his most refined manner, "Ladies and gentlemen, Miss Katharine Hepburn." From stage left, Audrey came downstage and smiled, bowing deeply. She didn't feel it was necessary to correct him. "I had been away so long I'm surprised they even got the last name right," she said. "Curiously, when I first met Hubert [Givenchy], I know he thought he was meeting the original Hepburn, Katharine Hepburn. But he was so gracious to me, this skinny little nobody."

She had arrived at his atelier in a simple T-shirt and a pair of slacks, but she left with visions of stunningly simple high-waisted suits and dresses in her favorite colors of black and white. Her love affair with his clothes never ended, but during the years she became a semi-recluse at Tolochenaz, she didn't dress up much. Her reentry into the world of formal dinners on the arm of Robbie also meant a trip through her closets, where the timeless designs still looked fabulous on her painfully svelte form.

Dressed in her beloved Givenchy, with a simple strand of good pearls and a pair of diamond earrings, she was always the most striking woman at any party. Her severe thinness, offset by that gigantic crooked smile, made Audrey seem regal yet approachable, a look that was genuinely representative of her nature.

She flew to New York and Los Angeles to honor Fred Astaire and Hubert de Givenchy, reacquainting herself with old friends in both places and introducing them all to Wolders. "I was beyond middle age," she recalled, "and it felt like I was going to my own coming-out parties."

Back in Switzerland, the Baroness became progressively more feeble. Audrey and Wolders took turns feeding her and keeping a bedside vigil. "I was extremely attached to my mother," Audrey said. "She was my lifeline. Her intelligence and bravery kept me alive during the war. I idolized her. She was not the most emotionally showy person — in fact, there were times I thought she was cold — but she loved me in her heart, and I knew that all along. She had been devastated by my father's abandonment, too, probably more than me, but she kept it to herself as best she could, to give me an example of strength.

"When she died at Tolochenaz in 1984, she had been living there full-time for at least a decade. I was lost without her. She was my sounding board, my conscience. Without Robbie, I'm not sure I could have survived her death. But he was there, too, and he had memories of her as well, so together, we talk about her a lot and it helps keep her presence alive."

But the next few years turned out to be difficult ones for Audrey. She had devoted so much time and attention to her mother that her days seemed empty once she didn't have her to nurse. She halfheartedly agreed to do a television movie with Robert Wagner, but *Love Among Thieves*, which aired on ABC in 1987, was poorly received. "Audrey Hepburn is done wrong again," wrote John Leonard in *New York* magazine.

For about three hours a day, she used her garden as therapy. She turned the soil and fertilized, weeded her beloved lilies of the valley, pruned her white roses. In an old pair of jeans and a big straw hat, she made sure her tomato plants had enough sun and water. But she was biding her time, trying to fill it with busywork to avoid feeling the pain of loss.

"I could have let it be known I wanted to return to films, and I would have been very busy. But the truth is, I didn't want to go back. I had no desire to return to that kind of work. I wanted to do something worthwhile. I feel funny even now phrasing it that way: 'worthwhile.' But I wanted to give back a little of my good fortune — share the wealth, so to speak.

"There were many charities that had asked for my help over the years. I discussed all of them with Robbie. He and I thrived on each other's company. I didn't want to take on more than I could handle, than our relationship could sustain. But he, too, felt it was time to start giving back. It's an urge that's selfish more than altruistic — you know you're going to feel better by helping others. It's a wonderful realization, and it hit both of us square between the eyes at about the same time."

Chapter 26

The woman who couldn't physically bear any more children decided to bear the burden of children around the world in 1988.

Audrey had always felt a profound connection to children, as if she were more on their wavelength than on adults'. She had this uncanny knack for making a face or a sound that would totally captivate the imagination of a child. The fact is, she could communicate without words.

Shirley MacLaine remembers that while making *The Children's Hour* with Audrey in 1962, Sean Ferrer was totally enthralled by his mother. "I just about stood on my head for that boy, and he only had eyes for his mummy. I usually can charm the pants off babies, but I met my match in Audrey. And she didn't even try! It just came naturally.

"She was a healer, too. If she saw someone suffering, she tried to take on their pain. She knew how to love. That's why her work with UNICEF was the perfect marriage. She couldn't stand the idea of children having pain."

Her involvement with the United Nations Children's Fund was a gradual development. Over the years, she had been asked to support various UN causes with her presence, and she had gladly given of her time. But Audrey wanted a more concrete involvement. She wanted to make a real connection with the children, instead of passively using her celebrity status to raise money and awareness.

"It all goes back to the war. We had really been starving. That hurts, you know — physically. It causes enormous pain, because it's a gigantic strain on the organs to operate without fuel.

"Of course, there's the emotional pain, too. I'm sure we all know about that, but somehow we ignore it as not quite real. Yet I'd like people to know about the physical pain. For a while we had nothing but tulip bulbs. Of course, they can be pulverized into a fine flour and you can make a tasty cake from it — provided, of course, you have the milk and eggs to go with it! If not, it's just a hopeful thought. Well, during the war that's what I had most of — a lot of hopeful thoughts — but not much real food.

"I am close to UNICEF because I had received UN aid as a child when the Allies

331

landed in Holland. [She received assistance from the United Nations Relief and Rehabilitation Administration, UNRRA, the precursor to UNICEF.] I think my first chocolate bars were from them!

"I was always grateful, but I didn't do anything about it. I kept it to myself. I really wasn't charity-minded at all, like some stars. I wasn't big on the benefit circuit."

Yet in 1971, she was persuaded by impresario Alexander Cohen to join a host of other celebrities in *A World of Love*, a film whose sole purpose was to raise money for UNICEF.

"I got a taste of just how many needy children there were all over the world from doing that movie. It was astounding to me, the kind of thing I would avoid knowing if I could! But once I learned that so many of the world's helpless are young, homeless, and hungry, I couldn't forget it."

After her mother's death, when Audrey realized the time was right for a real commitment to the children of the world, she prayed for the strength to carry out her mission. Always frail, she worried that traveling to remote corners of the globe would tax her delicate constitution and prevent her from achieving her goals. With Wolders solidly behind her, she decided she didn't have any choice but to sign on. "Robbie wanted me to go ahead, I know my mother would have been proud, so I decided to forge ahead."

Princess Catherine Aga Khan, wife of UNICEF commissioner Prince Sadruddin Aga Khan, remembers talking to Audrey at a UN reception in the mid-1980s. "She didn't want to take on more than she could handle, not out of fear of overextending herself, but more because she didn't want to let down the people who were counting on her. I think most celebrities would gladly have lent their name to the cause, but that would be it. Audrey, on the other hand, would not lend her name unless she could also promise her full commitment. She talked to me about it at length, and I could see she was really struggling with the decision.

"As a child, seeing suffering around her, that awakened her to compassion," the Princess said. "Instead of making her bitter, as it did some, it made her generous, giving. The surprising thing is that she was like that with everyone. Every gesture was gracious, even in the refugee camps of Somalia. She was never trying to impress anyone. She was just like that, an angel."

When she traveled to remote and impoverished countries, she packed only jeans and polo shirts. She and Wolders would do their best to sleep on the excruciatingly long plane trips, to prepare for the grueling hours in the field, meeting with the local care-givers and trying to greet as many children as they could. They were fact finders as well as good-will ambassadors, and Audrey often requested detailed information about the countries to which she was sent.

"Do you know how many street children there are in South America? All over the world? Even in America? But especially in South America and India? It's something like one hundred million who live and die in the streets. Contaminated water is the biggest killer of children. They die of dehydration caused by diarrhea, which is caused by them drinking the contaminated water."

"UNICEF's biggest challenge is to get clean water to children. Isn't it shocking? In the latter part of the twentieth century, there still isn't clean water? We're trying, though. And I thank God now that I had this film career and that it made me so well-known. Because it's now clear to me the reason I got famous all those years ago. It was to have this career, this new one. To be able to do something — a small thing, really — to help people."

During her five years with UNICEF, Audrey became progressively more single-minded about making a real difference in the lives she touched. Normally a fairly patient person, Audrey bridled at the slowness with which wells were dug and planting techniques introduced. She wanted to see immediate results. She wanted to see lives saved. The magnitude of the UNICEF projects often prevented swift action, yet after having witnessed the devastation, the waiting was intolerable for Audrey.

She relished in the concrete details of her work. During an interview for the book, she regaled me with UNICEF's accomplishments.

"Last year we provided fifty-two million schoolbooks for Bangladesh, and in the last eight years we have sunk two hundred fifty thousand tube wells. They are too poor to have a proper sanitation system. For a hundred dollars you can pierce a tube well and pump water. It's all done by local labor, but we provide the tubes, the pipes, and everything so that the water can be distributed with the proper sanitation."

She had done intermittent work for UNICEF throughout the 1980s, but she didn't make a formal commitment to come on as ambassador-at-large until 1988.

"Robbie encouraged me to make the connection a real one. 'You've been auditioning for this job your whole life,' he said. 'It's about time you make it official.' There was a lot of truth to that. I came from a home — a mother — who taught me first and foremost that I am secondary to other people. Service to others is what gives us meaning for ourselves. In the motion picture business, it's easy to forget your ideals. But I got out of the business, didn't do anything much for a while, and had a lot of time to reflect on what I believed. It came down to the fact that I honored in my heart what my mother taught me. It was time to put it into action. It was time to say yes to UNICEF."

From the moment she agreed to do the work, she had an impact. "The work that Audrey Hepburn did for UNICEF was imperative for us," said Lawrence E. Bruce, Jr., the president and CEO of the United States Committee for UNICEF. "Many people think that UNICEF gets a slice of the UN pie, which is not the case. The organization has to raise its funds each year, so fund-raising is an ongoing effort."

In the midst of her work with UNICEF she also agreed to host a six-part PBS series, *Gardens of the World*. These programs allowed her to share with a whole new audience her passion for both the aesthetic joy and the therapeutic value of bringing beautiful things to life.

"Audrey never considered herself a good

gardener," said Janis Blackschleger, executive producer of *Gardens of the World.*

"She liked to talk about how good she was at pulling weeds. But that's because she was just so modest.

"We all know Audrey Hepburn is a great legend. But what she was more than that was a great human being. When you were with her you felt prettier, better about yourself and your own possibilities. I just feel grateful she agreed to do the show, because I had a chance to get to know her."

"I was initially very skeptical," Audrey said. "I mean I grow tomatoes; I plant a few rosebushes. My garden is really an orchard. There are lots of fruit trees, a little bit of a proper garden with flowers, a cutting garden, and a vegetable patch. It's very messy, but I love it. I am not a real gardener by any wild stretch, so I didn't really feel qualified to host the show."

Again, Wolders went to work on her, convincing her that she would be a fine narrator. "Anytime my confidence flags, he can boost it," she said. And although she initially felt that a show about gardens might seem frivolous coming from an ambassador for starving children, Audrey began to see the real connection between children and the environment.

What clinched the deal is the fact that the shows were filmed during the summers, the one season when her UNICEF duties let up. She traveled to sixteen gardens in seven countries and fell in love with the Giardino di Ninfa, outside of Rome. Built on the site of an early medieval town that has crumbled through the centuries, it is full of roses, irises, tulips, and trees. "It is completely wild," Audrey said. "I thought I only loved the orderliness of an English garden, but I fell in love with the jumble near Rome. It's friendly, inviting. You don't feel you have to dress up to walk through it."

But it was at a Shinto shrine in Japan that Audrey came to a revelation about the connection between gardening and her work with UNICEF. "The Japanese worship nature. They never cut a tree, and if it falls, they let things grow over it, so that it can support life again. Even in Somalia and Ethiopia, people plant seeds, watch them grow if the conditions are right. It's so life-affirming.

"Gardening is the greatest tonic and therapy a human being can have. Even if you have only a tiny piece of earth, you can create something beautiful, which we all have a great need for. If we begin by respecting plants, it's inevitable we'll respect people."

Glenn Berenbeim, the scriptwriter of *Gar-*

dens of the World, recalled her overwhelming concern for all life after he visited her at Tolochenaz. "The happiest times were the meals," he said. "Audrey made these wonderful salads. She fed the dogs buttered toast, which it was clear they loved! It was clear during my stay that one didn't interrupt the joy of a meal for, say, a phone call."

But if one of the animals got sick, that was another matter. Tuppena, the Jack Russell terrier she gave to Wolders as his first pet, got something caught in his throat during Berenbeim's visit.

"I was amazed at Audrey and Robbie's concern," he recalled. "For forty minutes, everything stopped. They stayed with Tuppena until they were sure he was okay. You couldn't fake that kind of respect for life. Audrey was amazing to all who met her. She believed all life was a miracle. That's why she worked so hard with UNICEF."

Audrey's involvement in UNICEF transcended the charity cocktail party circuit where she felt "old stars are propped up for wealthy people to gawk at who must then pay — and pay dearly — for seeing the wrinkles up close!"

"Audrey knew herself perfectly — the qualities as well as the flaws," recalled Givenchy. "I had not dressed her for a film since she became devoted to UNICEF, but I continued to make some of her evening dresses and day wear. She once told me, 'When I talk about UNICEF in front of the television cameras, I am naturally emotional. Wearing your blouse makes me feel protected.' It was one of the most touching compliments she ever gave me," Givenchy said.

In her five active years with UNICEF, she made innumerable field trips to many of the one hundred twenty-eight countries the organization sponsors, including Bangladesh, the Sudan, Ethiopia, El Salvador, and Vietnam.

Wolders arranged for the trips, checking timetables and coordinating the numerous connecting flights. "I could never have done all of this work with UNICEF without Robbie," she said. "There's no way. Apart from my personal feelings, there's just no way the job could have been done. Robbie's on the phone the whole bloody time! He's the one who gets the flights, for free. UNICEF can't pay for hotels and other things. He's marvelous at it. Sometimes he cajoles airlines for UNICEF needs. He does a million things. When we get to a town where I have to speak the next day, he'll go and check the room and the mike, and he'll listen to what I'm going to say, and he'll tell me, 'No, that isn't right,' or 'It's okay,' or whatever. And we have each other to talk to."

A week after she joined UNICEF in 1988, she headed for Ethiopia, which was being ravaged by starvation and a civil war. "In the beginning, I knew my role was 'the lure.' Starvation in third-world countries was not hot copy," she said. "I think the powers-that-be rightly thought that I might be able to attract a little attention. All those reclusive years helped too! If I had been seen all over the place — except in my backyard in Switzerland, weeding — I wouldn't be quite the right snare. But laying low all those years made me a curiosity.

"When I finally accepted the job, I had no idea what I was getting into. The whole thing terrified me. It still does. Since we started, it's really been full-time. I don't mean every minute, or even every week, but while we're away in the countries we're busy from dawn to . . . well, dawn. We're on the go the whole time."

Although UNICEF officials would have been content if Audrey had functioned merely as a figurehead leader, that was never the case. From the moment she signed on, she went into the field, meeting with the starving children whose message of despair she hoped to carry to the rest of the world. She often slept in the refugee camps with the disenfranchised, sharing their meager meals with them. Completely hands-on in her approach, she raised the consciousness of millions of people about countries they never knew existed.

"Speaking to the officials and the delegates back at the United Nations is very important too. You have to be responsible. You can't just get up and say, 'Oh, I'm happy to be here, and I love children,' " she told the novelist and journalist Dominick Dunne in 1991. "No, that's not enough. It's not even enough to know there's been a flood in Bangladesh and seven thousand people lost their lives. Why the flood? What is their history? Why are they one of the poorest countries today? How are they going to survive? Are they getting enough help? What are the statistics? What are their problems?"

She held press conferences wherever she went to make sure newspapers carried reports of what she had learned and what she had witnessed. "I do not want to see Ethiopians digging graves for their children any longer," she emphasized. In El Salvador, she spoke the words of Gandhi: "Wars cannot be won by bullets, but only by bleeding hearts."

In 1991, President George Bush gave Audrey the highest honor any individual can receive in the United States — the Presidential

Medal of Freedom. "I will not rest until no child goes hungry," she said. "All is possible."

Madeline Eisner, a UNICEF official who accompanied Audrey on her last mission to Somalia in September of 1992, recalled that she wanted to visit as many refugee centers and clinics as was humanly possible. "She insisted on seeing the worst of the worst," Eisner said. "She didn't flinch. You could sense she felt it was her duty, and her destiny."

"I walked right into a nightmare," Audrey recalled about Somalia. "Ethiopia had been brutally bad, but Somalia was beyond belief. No stories in the press could prepare me for what I saw. The unspeakable agony of it! I kept seeing these countless little, fragile, emaciated children sitting under the trees, waiting to be fed. There wasn't food, yet they waited. Most of them were very ill — dying, I guess. I'll never forget their huge eyes in tiny faces and the terrible silence."

Somalia was indeed different.

Thanks in many ways to Audrey's tireless efforts and rare talent for using her glamour to focus the world's attention on its most destitute, Somalia was not to be forgotten. CNN, the TV networks, and the rest of the world's media brought home daily images of cruelty, carnage, and the haunting, sunken eyes of children starving slowly to death. Something had to be done.

In an unprecedented action, President Bush, in the waning days of his administration, dispatched thousands of U.S. troops to Somalia to quell the violence, restore civil order, and distribute food. Mass starvation came to an immediate halt. While the military and political implications of "Operation Restore Hope" have yet to be sorted out at this writing, the purely humanitarian motive of its mission marks a new chapter in the use of military power.

Audrey had moved millions with her movies. Now she had moved a president, a nation, and the world to action in what would be the last triumphant performance of her public career.

Audrey began to suffer debilitating stomach pain during her visit to Somalia, but she kept quiet about it. She did not want to jeopardize her visit to the ravaged African nation with personal concerns.

"I could sense that something was wrong with her," said Giovanni Brazzo, a United Nations aide who accompanied her on the trip to Somalia. "She was emaciated, as thin as the malnourished babies she was trying to help. But she got up as early as the rest of us, and she probably went to bed even later. 'There is so much to do,' she said, 'how can I be tired?' "

"A child is a child in any country, whatever the politics," she said simply. "Let's get down to basics. That's what a child forces you to do. Nothing else much matters, there is no complicated diplomacy, when a child is starving. It's simple. And we'd better do something about it. For our sakes, too. That is, if we want to continue to call ourselves human."

Chapter 27

"She was a star in France, England, the U.S., Italy," said Tolochenaz's mayor, Pierre-Alaine Mercier, on the day Audrey was buried. "She was a star throughout the whole world. But to me, she was just another neighbor. I used to see her working on her flowers like anyone else, and we'd say hello. Everyone knew the same thing about her: She was a person like any other — not at all a star."

Audrey would have adored Mercier's eulogy more than any other. She would have loved his tone and the matter-of-factness of his observations. She would have loved the acceptance in his words, the reality that she had become what she always wanted to be: someone's neighbor. Of course, in order to be a neighbor, you must live in a home. And her beloved home since 1966, La Paisible — "The Peaceful Place" — was, fittingly, the site of her death and her final resting place.

Colon cancer had been diagnosed in November of 1992, two months after her last visit to Somalia. She'd begun to have excruciating stomach pains while in Africa, and when she described her symptoms to doctors upon her return, they assumed she'd contracted an amoebic infection. Surgery in November pinpointed the cancer, but it had metastasized. Doctors opened her up and closed her. There was nothing they could do.

She flew back from Los Angeles, where she had received medical treatment, to Tolochenaz and her beloved stone farmhouse. The pain was unbearable, reported friend Henry Gris, but Audrey refused to succumb to it. She didn't wince, she didn't cry. Her expression remained peaceful, as if she were glad, at least, to be able to die in a place she loved.

As chance would have it, Audrey's final film role was as an angel. While Steven Spielberg's 1989 melodrama *Always* was neither a critical favorite nor a box office success, it allowed audiences one last look at Audrey Hepburn as Hap, an angel who shares her wisdom with Richard Dreyfuss. "Inspiration," she advises him, "that's the divine breath."

"It's what people count on. They reach for it, they pray for it. And quite often just when they need it most, they get it; it's breathed into them. And now it's your turn to give it back."

To her final days, Audrey never failed to inspire.

Friends rallied to her side. Doris Brynner, one of her closest pals, spent as much time as she could with Audrey in the final days. Of course, her beloved Wolders was with her day and night, and his overwhelming devotion never failed. Her sons Sean and Luca spent time trying to brighten her spirits, but found that she brightened theirs. The house took on an air of quiet festivity; people were coming in and out, the Jack Russell terriers were always barking. There was more action than there had been in years.

"She was so elegantly constructed and perfectly dressed that she made all other women look gross," said the author Judith Krantz. "Yet she escaped malice and envy because she was the quintessential waif. Under all that immaculate, cultivated style we sensed someone incredibly fragile, someone who, for reasons we never knew, seemed to need us. It was an incredible transference."

At the end, she left the world as she had lived in it: with grace and dignity. She died on January 20, 1993, with Wolders and her two sons at her side.

Four days later, mourners arrived at La Paisible, the home she had so often described as "everything I ever longed for." They passed through a simple white gate and still obeyed the unpretentious sign she had erected. In

French, it said: RING, AND ENTER, PLEASE.

And so they did. Commissioner of UNICEF Prince Sadruddin Aga Khan was one of the first to arrive. Actors Roger Moore and Alain Delon came soon afterward. Doris Brynner could not stem her tears and they streamed down her face during the whole ceremony.

It took place only a few hundred yards from Audrey's home in the Eglise de Tolochenaz, a simple, brown, stone church. A shaken, pale Mel Ferrer arrived with his fourth wife, Lise. He stood quietly at the sidelines, rhythmically squeezing his camel-colored gloves and biting his lip as if to hold back the tears. "Come, Papa," Sean called to his father. The two men tightly embraced one another before walking through the church portal. Rev. Maurice Eindiguer, the retired Episcopal minister who had married Hepburn and Ferrer in Burgenstock in 1954, conducted the short, moving service.

He cried, too, but silently, like so many of the mourners, who seemed intent on conducting themselves with the quiet aplomb of the woman they so loved. "Even in her illness," he said, "she visited those children in Somalia. She was a wonderful, giving lady who thought less of herself than anyone I ever met. She reached out to those dying children, year after year. A movie star? They didn't know that.

She was a lady who hugged them. And in their faces was a light reflected from her smile."

More than seven hundred townsfolk waited quietly outside the church to pay their last respects to their neighbor and friend, Madame Hepburn. They heard the sweet hymns being sung by a nearby girls' choir, and some of them joined in.

The graveyard was visible from the church. Audrey's casket, a simple blond oak, was carried by her sons, Sean and Luca; her beloved, Robbie Wolders; her ex-husband Andrea Dotti; and her dear friend Hubert de Givenchy. Ferrer, too frail to offer his assistance, walked nearby.

As she was laid to rest, friends threw white tulips into her grave. It was marked by a simple wooden cross that read: AUDREY HEPBURN 1929-1993. Next to the cross there is a small garden. But no one to tend it now.

"Last Christmas Eve," Sean said when he was asked to say a few words about his mother, "Mummy read a letter to us. [It said] 'If you ever need a helping hand, it's at the end of your arm. As you get older, you must remember you have a second hand. The first one is to help yourself; the second one is to help others.' "

Beneath that stunningly breathtaking exterior was the heart of a saint. It was a rare confluence of attributes. Audrey touched as many people with her kindness as she did with her beauty.

"I am and forever will be devastated by the gift of Audrey Hepburn before my camera," said photographer Richard Avedon. "In a way that was unique in my experience as a photographer, I loved her, but I always found her impossible to photograph.

"However you defined the encounter of the sexes, she won. I couldn't lift her to greater heights. She is already there. I could only record. I could not interpret her. There was no going further than who she was. She paralyzed me. She had achieved in herself the ultimate portrait.

"There was a moment between us she knows nothing of. I was walking one freezing evening in the Tuileries. I saw Audrey coming toward me. She was out with her dog. The way she moved through the low winter light, through the leafless trees, the absolute shadow she and the iced branches cast in my direction, stopped me dead — forced me to cross the path to avoid the flat-out immobilizing power of her presence. There was no way I could enter that perfect moment. She was already there."

Audrey finally achieved a perfection in her life that matched her outward and inward beauty. Her death, however untimely, however unfair, came at a time when she was doing exactly what she wanted — and when she finally knew what that was: working ceaselessly to help starving children, puttering around in her beloved garden, enjoying quiet times with Wolders and her two sons. Through hard work and good luck, she had exorcised the demons of insecurity that had plagued her youth.

In her last years, Audrey experienced unabashed joy. Having known her, I feel as grateful for that gift as I know she was. Because, simply put, the story of her life deserved a happy ending.